INTERNATIONAL SERIES IN
NATURAL PHILOSOPHY
SERIES EDITOR: D. TER HAAR

Volume 85

MECHANISMS OF
SPEECH RECOGNITION

Other Titles of interest:

MECHANISMS OF SPEECH RECOGNITION

BY

W. A. AINSWORTH

Department of Communication, University of Keele, Keele, Staffordshire

PERGAMON PRESS

OXFORD · NEW YORK · TORONTO
SYDNEY · PARIS · FRANKFURT

U.K.	Pergamon Press Ltd., Headington Hill Hall, Oxford, England
U.S.A.	Pergamon Press Inc., Maxwell House, Fairview Park, Elmsford, New York 10523, U.S.A.
CANADA	Pergamon of Canada, P.O. Box 9600, Don Mills M3C2T9, Ontario, Canada
AUSTRALIA	Pergamon Press (Aust.) Pty. Ltd., 19a Boundary Street, Rushcutters Bay, N.S.W. 2011, Australia
FRANCE	Pergamon Press SARL, 24 rue des Ecoles, 75240 Paris, Cedex 05, France
WEST GERMANY	Pergamon Press GmbH, 6242 Kronberg/Taunus, Pferdstrasse 1, Frankfurt-am-Main, West Germany

First edition 1976

Library of Congress Cataloging in Publication Data

Ainsworth, William Anthony.
Mechanisms of speech recognition.

(International series in natural philosophy)
(Pergamon international library of science, technology, engineering, and social studies; v. 85)
1. Speech perception. 2. Speech–Physiological aspects. I. Title. [DNLM: 1. Auditory perception. 2. Speech. WV501 A297m]
QP464.A36 1976 612'.85 76-912
ISBN 0-08-020395-7
ISBN 0-08-020394-9 pbk.

Printed in Great Britain by A. Wheaton & Co. Exeter

Contents

Foreword

The study of speech is a multidisciplinary subject, and the topic of this book is no exception. The production of speech is properly the province of the anatomist and the physiologist, but in practice it has been studied mainly by the phonetician with help from the physicist. The sounds of speech have been classified by the phonetician, and analysed by him with instrumental help from the telecommunications engineer.

The hearing mechanism is studied by the physiologist both for its own intrinsic interest and in the hope that a better understanding of the mechanism may lead to cures for some forms of deafness. The perception of sound is a subject for the psychologist, and latterly for the psychophysicist. The sub-branch of this topic with which this book is concerned, however, commands a wider audience. It requires a phonetician, a linguist, a physiologist, a psychologist and a physicist for a full appreciation of its problems and interests.

It is the hope of the writer that those who are interested in the topic of speech recognition, and especially those who possess skills in any of the above disciplines, will find that the information in this book stimulates them to study the other relevant disciplines so that a more comprehensive viewpoint can be achieved. It is also hoped that those with knowledge of some of the topics discussed will pardon the errors and omissions, and not let these prevent them from reading those chapters where the subject matter is less familiar.

I should like to acknowledge my indebtedness to all those friends and colleagues who have contributed, either directly or indirectly, to my knowledge of the subject. They are too numerous to mention, but most of their names appear in the list of references. My apologies to those I have missed.

Finally I must add that without the help of my wife this book would never have been completed.

June 1975   W. A. AINSWORTH

CHAPTER 1

Speech Production

Introduction

During the last few centuries enormous advances have been made in our understanding of the physical world in which we live. We can predict the behaviour of inanimate objects with great precision, and can manipulate this behaviour for our own purposes.

Our understanding of the animate world, however, has not reached anything like such an advanced state. The reasons for this are threefold. Firstly, there is the attitude of mind from which we approach the subject. We are animate objects ourselves, and if we ignore this fact our understanding will be very limited. If we predict the behaviour of a person and he knows that his behaviour is being predicted, this knowledge may alter his behaviour in such a way that the original prediction is falsified. Secondly, a knowledge of the physical properties of the materials of which the animate objects are composed is a prerequisite of a complete understanding of such objects. Thirdly, the complexity of animate objects is in general enormous compared with inanimate objects, and the interdependency of their parts is vastly greater.

Whilst reasons of the first type are still valid, many of the problems have been overcome by adopting an information processing point of view towards animate objects, and by posing questions in relative rather than absolute terms. Reasons of the second and third types are gradually being eliminated. Our knowledge of the physical properties of the component parts of animate objects is continually advancing, and techniques for dealing with more and more complex systems are gradually being evolved. A greater understanding of the animate world is thus being acquired.

A particular area of interest to both the physical scientist and the behavioural scientist is sensory perception: how are the shapes and motions of the physical world transformed into the sights and sounds of the mind? In this book we will be concerned with one branch of this subject which is particularly important for human beings: speech recognition.

At the physical level, speech is just a particular type of acoustic signal. Its production can be explained in terms of the resonances of the vocal tract, and it can be analysed by conventional methods into its component frequencies. Furthermore, it can be transmitted over great distances, virtually undistorted, by techniques developed by electrical engineers. At this level speech is well understood.

Once its interaction with the hearing mechanism is considered, however, some of the associated phenomena become a little more difficult to explain. Speech which is buried in noise can be understood surprisingly well, and a conversation in a crowded room, in which several other equally loud conversations are taking place, can readily be followed.

1

At the next level, when the sounds of speech have been transformed into neural activity by the mechanism of the inner ear, the mystery deepens and the similarities between speech and other sounds begin rapidly to disappear. It is becoming clear that different parts of the brain are employed for the analysis of speech and non-speech sounds, and some experiments have been interpreted as suggesting that one ear is better for perceiving speech and the other is better for perceiving other sounds!

Speech communication

It is essential to recognize at the outset that speech recognition is part of a communication process. The aim of the communication process is to transmit an idea in the mind of the speaker to the mind of the listener. This is achieved by the speaker formulating the idea in words, then encoding this message in sounds by means of his speech production mechanism. These sounds are transmitted to the listener as an acoustic signal. There they are transformed into neural activity by the listener's hearing mechanism, recognized as speech, then decoded into the message by the listener's brain. This process is only successful if the speaker and the listener have a language in common.

Little is yet known about how an idea is formulated as a message, and this process is anyway beyond the scope of this book. We will begin by examining the way in which the organs of the vocal apparatus are employed to transform a message consisting of a string of linguistic units, such as words or phonemes, into a wave of continuous sounds which we recognize as speech. Speech recognition is the process of decoding this continuous acoustic wave into a string of linguistic units from which the intended message can be deduced. In order to understand this process we need to know something of the auditory mechanism, both of its physical properties and its behaviour in a variety of circumstances, and of the features of the acoustic wave which are important for the decoding process.

Phonemes

It is useful to describe spoken utterances by strings of discrete elements representing the sounds which have been produced, although in natural speech the boundaries between these elements are often impossible to place. A convenient unit for these elements is the "phoneme". This is a linguistic unit defined such that if one phoneme is substituted for another the meaning of the word may be changed. The set of phonemes employed in each language is thus different. In English /l/ and /r/ are two distinct phonemes (lead /lɛd/ has a different meaning from red /rɛd/), whereas in Japanese they are not. In this book the phonemes of English will be used, and where there is no doubt, and nothing is said to the contrary, of British English. In order to distinguish the phonetic symbols from the orthographic letters, the phonetic symbols will be written between oblique lines.

The phonemes of English are shown in Fig. 1.1 and examples of words in which they are used are given in Table 1.1. Many of the vowels and some of the consonants are commonly denoted by alternative symbols. The /ʃ/ symbol, for example, which represents ("sh" in "ship" /ʃɪp/) is sometimes shown as /š/. The so-called "long"

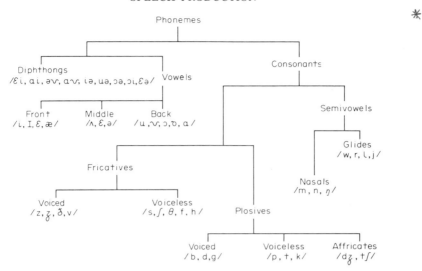

Fig. 1.1. The phonemes of British English.

vowels are often shown as such specifically by following their representation by a colon-like symbol; thus "seat" may be transcribed as /si:t/. In this book, however, the single symbol notation shown in Table 1.1 will be adhered to.

Vocal apparatus

The apparatus used for producing speech probably evolved primarily for two other purposes: breathing and eating. The muscular activity necessary for speaking must be learned.

A diagram of the vocal apparatus is shown in Fig. 1.2. It consists of the lungs, trachea (windpipe) and the oral and nasal tracts. In the process of breathing air is drawn into the lungs by expanding the rib cage and lowering the diaphragm. This reduces the pressure in the lungs and air flows in, usually via the nostrils, nasal tract and trachea. The air is normally expelled by the same route. During eating the food is prevented from entering the trachea by the epiglottis. When food is swallowed the esophagus, which normally lies collapsed against the back of the throat, is opened to provide a passage to the stomach.

In speaking the lungs are filled with air as in breathing, except that the oral tract as well as the nasal tract is used. When the lungs are filled, the pressure is increased by contracting the rib cage. This increase in pressure forces the air from the lungs into the pharynx. At the top of the trachea is a structure known as the larynx. This houses two lips of ligament, called the vocal cords or folds. Situated between them is a slit-like orifice, the glottis, which is opened by the pressure of air. As the air flow builds up the local pressure is reduced by the Bernoulli effect, and the tension in the cords draws them together. As the glottis closes the pressure again builds up, forcing the cords apart, and the cycle is repeated. This process is known as "phonation".

The pulses of air so produced excite the resonating cavities of the oral and nasal

Table 1.1. Pronunciation of the Phonemes of English.

Phoneme	Class	Example
/b/	Voiced plosives	*b*at
/d/		*d*og
/g/		*g*et
/p/	Voiceless plosives	*p*ig
/t/		*t*ell
/k/		*k*ick
/m/	Nasals	*m*an
/n/		*n*ull
/ŋ/		si*ng*
/w/	Glides	*w*ell
/r/		*r*an
/l/		*l*et
/j/		*y*ou
/h/	Voiceless fricatives	*h*at
/f/		*f*ix
/θ/		*th*ick
/s/		*s*at
/ʃ/		*sh*ip
/v/	Voiced fricatives	*v*an
/ð/		*th*is
/z/		*z*oo
/ʒ/		a*z*ure
/dʒ/	Affricates	*j*oke
/tʃ/		*ch*ew
/i/	Front vowels	s*ea*t
/ɪ/		b*i*t
/ɛ/		h*ea*d
/æ/		h*a*t
/ɑ/	Back vowels	c*a*rt
/ʊ/		r*o*d
/ɔ/		c*o*rd
/ᴜ/		w*ou*ld
/u/		r*u*de
/ɜ/	Middle vowels	d*i*rt
/ʌ/		h*u*t
/ə/		th*e*

tracts. In non-nasalized sounds the velum is positioned to prevent any flow of air through the nasal tract. In such a case the sound will radiate from the lips. In nasal sounds the lips are closed, the velum is positioned to allow air to flow through the nasal tract and the sound radiates from the nostrils. The rate at which the vocal cords vibrate depends upon the pressure in the lungs and the tension in the vocal cords. Both of these are under the control of the speaker, and can be adjusted to vary the pitch of the sound produced. Sounds generated in this manner with the larynx phonating are known as

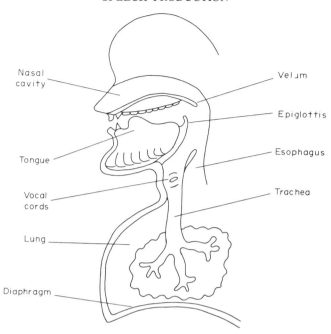

Fig. 1.2. The vocal apparatus.

voiced sounds. Other sounds, the voiceless sounds, are produced by a turbulent flow of air caused by a constriction at some point in the vocal tract. This constriction may be formed by the lips, the tongue or the velum.

Another source of excitation can be created by closing the vocal tract at some point, allowing the pressure to build up, and then suddenly releasing it. This form of excitation is employed in the production of plosive consonants.

Whispered speech is produced by partially closing the glottis so that turbulent flow replaces the periodic excitation (phonation) during normally voiced sounds.

Production of vowels

The vowels are produced by voiced excitation of the oral tract. During the articulation of a vowel the tract normally maintains a relatively stable shape and, in English, the velum is normally closed to prevent excitation of the nasal tract. In some other languages, such as French, some of the vowels are deliberately nasalized.

The oral tract may be considered to be a tube about 17 cm long, closed at the source end (the glottis) and open at the other end (the lips). Its cross-section area is small compared with its length, so plane acoustic waves propagate in the tract. These waves may be described by the sound pressure, p, and the volume velocity, u, as functions of distance along the tract from the glottis.

The effect of the open end on the sound in the tube can be represented by radiation impedance. At low frequencies this consists of a resistance $\rho c / A$ in parallel with an acoustic mass, $m \simeq 0.4\rho A^{1/2}$, where A is the cross-sectional area, ρ the density of the air and c the velocity of sound (Stevens and House, 1961).

If p_r is the pressure at the distance r from the mouth and u_o is the volume velocity at the mouth opening, then the radiation of the sound from the mouth is given by

$$R(j\omega) = p_r(j\omega)/u_o(j\omega)$$

where $\omega = 2\pi f$ is the radian frequency of the sound. For a point source, it has been shown by Morse (1948) that

$$R(j\omega) = j\omega\rho/4\pi r.$$

The transfer function of the vocal tract is given by

$$T(j\omega) = u_o(j\omega)/u_s(j\omega)$$

where $u_s(j\omega)$ is the volume velocity of the source. Hence the sound pressure at a distance r from the lips during the production of a vowel can be considered the product of three terms:

$$p_r(j\omega) = u_s(j\omega) \quad T(j\omega) \quad R(j\omega).$$

The different vowels are produced by the speaker manipulating his articulators in order to change the transfer function $T(j\omega)$.

In articulatory phonetics the vowels are characterized by the positions of the articulators. If the jaw drops so that the vocal tract is wide, the vowel is said to be "open", and if the vocal tract is narrow the vowel is "close". Another dimension is the position of the tongue hump. If this is at the back of the mouth the vowel is said to be "back", and if it is at the front it is a "front" vowel.

One way of describing a vowel is by its position on a vowel quadrilateral (Fig. 1.3). The vowels represented by the extremes of the quadrilateral are known as the "cardinal" vowels (Jones, 1949). Other vowels are judged according to their likeness to these vowels, and placed accordingly on the chart. The vowels of English, when spoken as isolated syllables, assume approximately the positions shown in Fig. 1.3. This type of chart enables phoneticians to compare the vowels occurring in different languages.

A third dimension, duration, is sometimes employed in the description of vowels. The vowels /i, æ, ɜ, u, ɔ, ɑ/ are the long vowels, whilst /ɪ, ɛ, ʊ, ʌ, ɒ, ə/ are short. In continuous speech, however, duration depends on the adjacent consonants and the stress on the syllable as well as on the intrinsic duration.

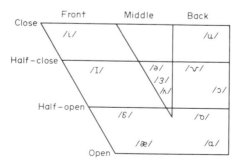

Fig. 1.3. The vowel quadrilateral.

To return to the acoustics of vowel production, a rigid tube can be considered as a loss-less resonator represented by a capacitance, C, and inductance, L, in parallel as shown in Fig. 1.4. This will have a resonance at a frequency F1 given by

$$F1 = \tfrac{1}{2}\pi(LC)^{\frac{1}{2}}.$$

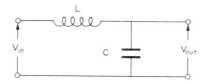

Fig. 1.4. Electrical equivalent of a lossless resonator.

Flanagan (1965) has shown that for a uniform tube of length l and cross-sectional area A

$$C = Al/\rho c^2 \quad \text{and} \quad L = \rho l/A.$$

Substituting $l = 17$ cm for the length of a male vocal tract, 1.14×10^{-3} g/cm^3 for the density of air, and 3.5×10^4 cm/sec for the velocity of sound in air, F1 $\simeq$ 300 Hz. This is near to the frequency of the first resonance in the /u/ vowel.

In a real physical system there will be losses through the walls of the vocal tract. The transfer function is then given by

$$T(j\omega) = \frac{s_1 s_1^*}{(j\omega - s_1)(j\omega - s_1^*)}$$

where $s_1 + \sigma_1 + j\omega_1$, $s_1^* = \sigma_1 - j\omega_1$, $\omega_1 = 2\pi$F1, and σ_1 is a constant which depends on the amount of dissipation. The complex numbers s_1 and s_1^* are the poles of the transfer function.

A vocal tract, however, is not a simple resonator. It is more like a transmission line. The wave is reflected back from the opening at the mouth, interfering with the wave from the source. Such a system has an infinite number of resonances with the transfer function given by

$$T(j\omega) = \frac{s_1 s_1^*}{(j\omega - s_1)(j\omega - s_1^*)} \cdot \frac{s_2 s_2^*}{(j\omega - s_2)(j\omega - s_2^*)} \cdots \frac{s_n s_n^*}{(j\omega - s_n)(j\omega - s_n^*)}$$

where $s_i = \sigma_i + j\omega_i$, etc., are the poles of the function (Fant, 1960).

For a uniform tube, open at one end and closed at the other, the modes of vibration are shown in Fig. 1.5. The wavelength λ of each mode is given by

$$\lambda = 4l/(2n + 1).$$

$$\text{Now } \lambda = c/f, \quad \text{so } f_n = (2n + 1)c/4l.$$

A neutral vowel /ə/ is reproduced with the vocal tract configuration near to a uniform tube. Its resonances are, therefore, about 500, 1500, 2500 Hz, etc.

The energy spectrum of the source, however, falls with increasing frequency at about 12 dB/octave, so only the first few resonances can be observed in the waveform.

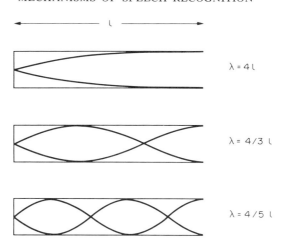

Fig. 1.5. Resonances in a uniform tube, open at one end and closed at the other.

Diphthongs

The diphthongs are produced in a similar manner to the vowels, except that the shape of the vocal tract changes during articulation. The acoustics of their production is thus similar to vowels, but the cross-sectional area of the vocal tract at each point is gradually changing.

The phonemic symbols used to represent the diphthongs reflect their similarity to vowels in that the first element represents the vocal tract shape at the start of the diphthong and the second element the shape at the end. For example, the diphthong /ɑi/ is produced by changing from an open-back shape, /ɑ/, to a close-front one, /i/.

In practice these shapes are only approximated. In continuous speech the first part of the diphthong may match the ideal form reasonably well, but the second part will probably consist of a gesture of the articulators in the direction appropriate for the second part of the diphthong.

Table 1.2 shows the diphthongs employed by a speaker of RP (Received Pronunciation—a non-regional British English dialect). The elements of these

Table 1.2. The diphthongs
of RP English

Phoneme	Example
εi	pay
ɑi	high
ɔʋ	road
ɑʋ	cow
iə	hear
uə	endure
ɔə	sore
ɔi	boy
εə	care

diphthongs should be taken to represent only the directions of movement of the articulators. Diphthongs, even more than vowels, are notoriously dependent on the dialect of the speaker. The diphthong /əʊ/, as in "hole", is articulated as /ɛʊ/ by a speaker from the South-east and as near /uʌ/ by a speaker from parts of Scotland.

Nasals

The nasals are produced by positioning the velum so that the nasal tract is excited by the pulses of air from the larynx. The oral tract is closed at some point. The acoustics of nasal production can be calculated by considering a tube closed at the source end (glottis) and open at the other end (nostrils), but with a closed side branch (mouth) as shown in Fig. 1.6.

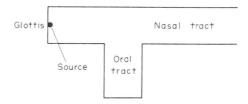

Fig. 1.6. Configuration of the vocal tract for the production of nasals.

The point of closure determines the length of the side tube, and hence the frequency at which the oral tract will resonate. If the oral tract is closed at the lips, an /m/ sound is produced. When the tongue is placed against the roof of the mouth in order to close the tract, an /n/ sound is generated. When the velum is used to close the oral tract an /ŋ/ sound results. This latter sound only occurs in post-vowel position in English.

Semivowels

The semivowels, or glides, are produced in a similar manner to the vowels and diphthongs. The larynx phonates and the air flows through the oral tract. During the production of these phonemenes the articulators move more rapidly than in the production of diphthongs. For a /j/ the vocal tract is in its close position as though an /i/ vowel was about to be articulated, but the tract opens and the tongue moves quickly to the position appropriate for the vowel which follows the /j/. Similarly a /w/ is produced with the lips rounded and the tract positioned for an /u/ vowel, but the articulators move rapidly and this position is only held instantaneously.

The /r/ and /l/ are produced in a similar fashion except that there are no vowels in English which have the same tract shapes as their starting positions. The characteristic of /l/ is a very rapid movement of the tip of the tongue from somewhere near the tooth ridge. In /r/ the tongue also moves from the roof of the mouth but at a slightly slower rate. The point at which the tongue tip makes contact with the roof of the mouth for an /l/ in post-vowel position depends somewhat on the vowel which it follows.

Fricatives

In the production of fricatives the articulatory configuration is characterized by a rather narrow constriction, the position of which depends on the particular consonant. Air is forced through this constriction, and turbulent flow occurs. Noise is generated as a result of this turbulent flow, which excites the resonances of the cavities of the vocal tract.

As the constriction may occur at a number of places in the vocal tract, the acoustic model will consist of a noise source exciting two tubes, one closed representing the portion of the vocal tract prior to the constriction and one open representing the portion of the vocal tract between the constriction and the lips (Fig. 1.7).

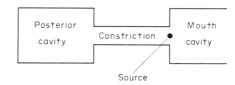

Fig. 1.7. Configuration of the vocal tract for the production of voiceless fricatives.

The noise source will excite the natural resonances of both of these tubes. At frequencies equal to the resonances of the lower part of the vocal tract, the energy of the source at these frequencies will be absorbed by this part of the system, so the spectrum of the signal at the lips will contain zeros as well as poles. The transfer function of the vocal tract during the production of fricatives is thus proportional to

$$\prod_i \frac{s_i^*}{(j\omega - s_i)(j\omega - s_i^*)} \cdot \prod_j \frac{(j\omega - s_j)(j\omega - s_j^*)}{s_j s_j^*}$$

where s^* is the complex conjugate of s, s_i are the poles, and s_j are the zeros of the transfer function (Heinz and Stevens, 1961).

The unvoiced fricatives /f,θ, s,ʃ/ are well described by this model. The voiced fricatives /v,ð,z,ʒ/ are a little more complex. In addition to the "source" at the constriction, there is another (periodic) source at the glottis. The model is more like that shown in Fig. 1.8.

An /f/ and a /v/ are articulated by placing the upper front teeth against the lower lip. In the case of /v/ the larynx phonates at the same time. A /θ/ and a /ð/ are generated by

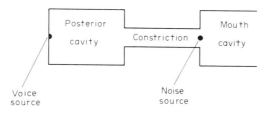

Fig. 1.8. Configuration of the vocal tract for the production of voice fricatives.

placing the tongue against the upper teeth, /s/ and /z/ by placing the upper and lower rows of teeth together and the tongue tip near the tooth ridge, and /ʃ/ and /ʒ/ by placing the tongue near the roof of the mouth and rounding the lips.

The phoneme /h/ may be considered to belong to the class of voiceless fricatives as it is also produced by a constriction in the vocal tract. In this case the constriction is at the glottis with the cords held slightly open (rather than fully open as with a normal fricative) but not vibrating. The acoustic model is rather like that of the vowels with the source at the closed end (glottis) of the tube, but with an aperiodic rather than periodic source. The sound radiating from the lips depends on the transfer function (and thus the shape) of the vocal tract as with vowel sounds.

Plosives

Plosives, or stop consonants, are generated by closing the vocal tract completely for a short time, allowing the pressure to build up, then releasing it suddenly. The stop consonants are distinguished by the place at which the vocal tract is closed, and by the manner of their release (voiced or unvoiced). The bilabial stops, /b/ and /p/, are produced by closure at the lips. If the vocal cords begin vibrating at or before the instant of release, the voiced stop /b/ is produced, but if there is a significant delay a /p/ is generated. If closure is produced by placing the tongue against the tooth ridge one of the alveolar stops, /d/ or /t/, is generated. Closure by means of the velum produces the velar stops, /g/ and /k/.

Closure at the glottis produces a glottal stop. This has no phonemic significance in English but it is, nevertheless, substituted for some of the other stops in some dialects.

Affricates

When a stop consonant is followed by a fricative, both are shortened, and they combine to form a single consonant known as an affricate. There are two of them in English. A voiced affricate, /dʒ/, and a voiceless one, /tʃ/. The motions of the articulators which generate these sounds are approximately those which would be expected from their phonemic representation.

Conclusions

The preceding paragraphs give a brief description of the movements of the articulators and the resulting acoustic changes involved in the production of speech sounds. This is something which every speaker of a language already knows, but perhaps in a less explicit form. More detailed descriptions of speech production may be found in any manual of phonetics (for example, Gimson, 1970, Brosnahan and Malmberg, 1970, or O'Connor, 1973).

In the speech communication process the "message" is encoded by the motion of the articulators into the vibrations of the speech wave. The mechanisms of the hearing system which detect and decode these vibrations will be considered in the subsequent chapters.

CHAPTER 2

The Auditory System

The sounds of speech, like all other audible sounds, are transmitted to the brain by means of the ears and the auditory nerve. The ear consists of three parts: the outer, middle, and inner ears. The outer ear is made up of the pinna (the external part on the side of the head) and the meatus (the external canal) which terminates at the eardrum. The middle ear contains the ossicles (the hammer, anvil, and stirrup) which transmit the vibrations of the eardrum to the oval window of cochlea. The inner ear contains the cochlea whose function is to analyse these vibrations and transform them into nerve impulses for transmission to the brain (Fig. 2.1).

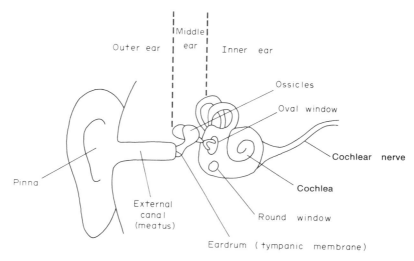

Fig. 2.1. Schematic diagram of the parts of the ear.

Outer ear

The function of the pinna is to protect the entrance to the external canal. Its shape makes it directionally sensitive at high frequencies, so it may also help in the location of sound sources. The external canal leads from the pinna to the middle ear. It is a tube about 2.7 cm in length and 0.7 cm in diameter. It is open at one end, and terminated at the other by the eardrum, or tympanic membrane. This is a relatively stiff cone with an angle at the apex of about 135°. Sound waves entering the ear impinge upon the tympanic membrane and cause it to vibrate.

12

Middle ear

The middle ear is an air-filled cavity which contains the ossicles. Its function is to transform the vibrations of the tympanic membrane into oscillations of the liquid in the inner ear. As the mechanical impedance of this liquid is much greater than that of the eardrum, a system of mechanical levers is required. This is achieved by a group of bones known as the ossicles.

The malleus, or hammer, is attached to the tympanic membrane, so when this membrane vibrates the malleus vibrates as well. The malleus makes contact with the incus, or anvil, causing it to rotate. The stapes, or stirrup, is connected to the incus, and its footplate is attached to the oval window, the entrance to the inner ear. As the effective area of the stapes is much less than that of the tympanic membrane, vibrations of the membrane are duplicated at the oval window even though the impedance of the window is much higher.

Another important function of the ossicles is to protect the delicate inner ear from damage caused by very loud sounds. In detailed studies of the vibrations of the ossicles, von Békésy (1960) observed that for sounds of low intensity the motion of the ossicles causes a pumping action of the stapes at the oval window, whereas for higher intensity sounds, near and above the threshold of feeling, the motion of the stapes is more of a rotation so that the amplitude of the oscillations is not increased proportionally to the increase of that of the oscillations of the tympanic membrane. A further protective function is probably provided by muscles attached to the eardrum which contract and attenuate the amplitude of the oscillations of the membrane.

Inner ear

The inner ear comprises the cochlea, the organ which transforms the mechanical vibrations into nerve impulses. It consists of a coiled structure containing two channels separated by the cochlear partition. Its structure is shown uncoiled in Fig. 2.2. It is about 35 mm long with a cross-sectional area of about 4 mm² at the stapes end and tapering to about 1 mm² at the tip. It is filled with a colourless liquid called perilymph.

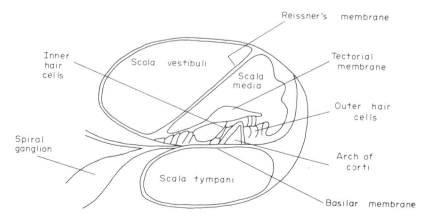

Fig. 2.2. Schematic cross-section through the cochlear canal.

The half of the cochlea which connects with the oval window is called the scala vestibuli, whilst the other half is called the scala tympani. The cochlea partition is itself a channel filled with a liquid called endolymph. It is bounded by the basilar membrane and Reissner's membrane (Fig. 2.3). These membranes terminate about a millimetre

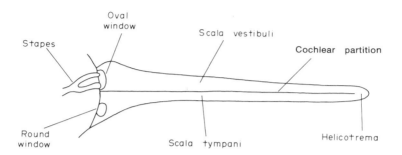

Fig. 2.3. Simplified diagram of an uncoiled cochlea.

short of the ends of the scalae, so the perilymph can flow between them at the helicotrema.

Attached to the basilar membrane is the organ of Corti, the complex of hair cells and supporting structures which perform the mechanical to neural transduction. The organ of Corti contains some 30,000 sensory cells. These transmit a description of the motion of the basilar membrane.

When a sound enters the ear it impinges upon the eardrum causing it to vibrate. These vibrations are transmitted to the inner ear by the ossicles. At very low frequencies (less than 20 Hz) the motion of the stapes causes the perilymph to flow from the scala vestibuli into the scala tympani via the helicotrema. The extra pressure in the scala tympani is relieved by expansion of a membrane in the round window. At higher frequencies of vibration, the pressure difference across the cochlea partition causes the basilar membrane to vibrate in a travelling wave pattern (von Békésy, 1960).

The basilar membrane tapers towards its apex, so its resonating properties vary along its length. The amplitudes of vibration at various positions along the membrane have been measured by von Békésy for a range of stimulating frequencies. They are shown approximately in Fig. 2.4. The amplitude and phase response of a given membrane point is like that of a broad band-pass filter. The amplitude responses of successive points have an approximate constant Q characteristic, the width of the filter being roughly proportional to its position in the membrane. As the frequency of vibration of the stapes is raised, the point of maximum oscillation of the basilar membrane moves nearer to the base of the cochlea.

The oscillations of the basilar membrane cause the hairs of the sensory cells to bend, which in turn cause nerve impulses to be sent up the auditory nerve. The cochlea thus performs a continuous broad-band analysis of the sounds which enter the ear, and transmits the results to the brain.

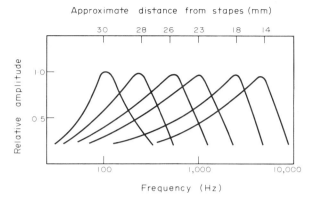

Fig. 2.4. Relative response of various points along the basilar membrane as a function of stimulus frequency.

Organ of Corti

The organ of Corti transforms the mechanical signals into electrical signals. A cross-section showing its structure is given in Fig. 2.5. The hair cells are attached to the basilar membrane, and are supported by the recticula laminae and other cells. The ends of the hairs are attached to the tectorial membrane. When the basilar membrane oscillates the hairs are bent and straightened. There are two sets of hair cells. The row which is nearest to the axis of the cochlea spiral comprises the inner hair cells. There are some 5000 of these. Towards the periphery of the cochlea spiral are three or four more rows, the outer hair cells. It has been estimated that there are about 25,000 of these. Davis (1958) found that the outer hair cells are sensitive to a bending motion across the basilar membrane, whereas the inner hair cells react to a motion along the basilar membrane. The mechanism by which the bending of the hair activates the nerve cells is not known, but presumably a potential is generated which is sufficient to fire the cell.

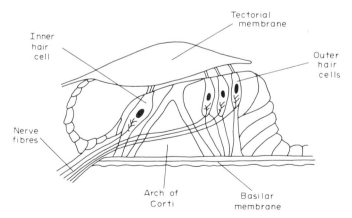

Fig. 2.5. Schematic diagram of the organ of Corti showing the inner and outer hair cells.

Nerve cells

There are many types of nerve cells, or neurones, in the brain, but they mostly consist of a cell body with an axon and dendrites as shown in Fig. 2.6. Each cell acts as

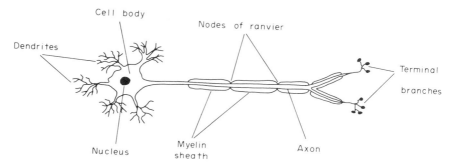

Fig. 2.6. Some of the parts of a neurone.

a relay station. Impulses from neighbouring cells are transmitted to the cell body by the dendrites. If there is sufficient activity, the impulses exceed the excitation threshold of the cell and the cell fires. An impulse of about a millisecond duration is transmitted down the axon at a steady velocity. The dendrites of other cells may be joined by synapses to this axon, and may in turn be triggered by this activity. On the other hand, they may be joined by inhibiting connections which prevent the cell from firing even though there is neural activity in the region of its dendrites. Once a cell has fired it takes a while before the cell can be fired again. This interval is known as the refractory period.

Neurones can act as transmitters of activity from peripheral sensory cells to the central regions of the brain. As the impulse is regenerated by an electrochemical process at each instant along the axon, the signals can be transmitted over relatively long distances with no attenuation. The speed of transmission depends on the thickness of the axon, so neurones may act as delay lines.

The probability of a neurone firing depends on the amount by which the activity reaching the cell body exceeds a threshold. This threshold might be such that a neurone will fire if two or more neighbouring neurones fire simultaneously. Neurones may thus act as coincidence detectors or as logic elements.

Pathways in the auditory system

The main ascending pathways from the cochlea to the auditory cortex are shown in Fig. 2.7. The dendrites of the first-order neurones are in contact with the hair cells of the organ of Corti. In general, the inner hair cells are served by only one or two neurones, and the outer hair cells by several. The cell bodies of the first-order neurones are located in the spiral ganglion, and their axons pass via the cochlear nerve to the dorsal and ventral nuclei in the medulla. The synapses of the second-order neurones are located here.

It will be seen that there are two parallel pathways, each leading to parts of the

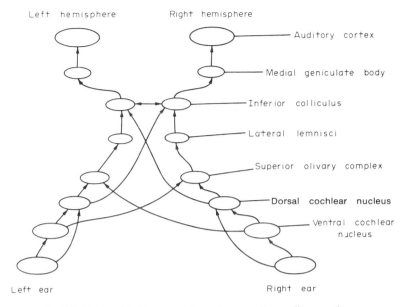

Fig. 2.7. Schematic diagram of the main ascending auditory pathways.

auditory cortex in different hemispheres of the brain. Some of the second-order neurones from the cochlear nuclei remain on the same side of the brain as the ear from which they originated, but most cross over to the lateral lemnisci on the opposite sides. From these, the pathways lead to the inferior colliculi. Here, at the level of the midbrain, there is again some interaction between the pathways.

From the inferior colliculi the pathways lead to the medial geniculate bodies, and thence to the auditory cortex.

Single unit recording

Using microelectrode techniques it is possible to monitor the activity of a single nerve cell. Some years ago tungsten electrodes having a tip diameter of about 1 micron were used to penetrate nerve cells (Hubel, 1957). More recently micropipettes filled with KCl solution have been preferred (Evans, 1972). Such electrodes have been employed to study the behaviour of various parts of the auditory system of guinea pigs (Tasaki, 1954; Evans, 1970), cats (Kiang *et al.*, 1965; Katsuki *et al.*, 1959; Evans and Whitfield, 1964) and monkeys (Katsuki *et al.*, 1962; Rhode, 1971).

Normally the animal is anaesthetized, and the part of the auditory system to be examined is exposed by surgery. A stainless-steel electrode is inserted into the muscles of the neck of the animal to act as an earth, and the microelectrode is inserted stereotactically into the nerve cells of the region of interest. The sound stimulus is applied, and the spikes discharged by the neurone at the tip of the microelectrode are detected. The discharge pattern is amplified, and passed to the recording apparatus or to a digital computer for analysis. A typical discharge pattern for an active cell is shown in Fig. 2.8.

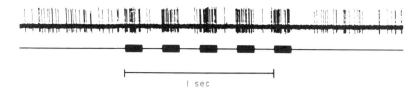

Fig. 2.8. Response of a neurone (upper trace) to a series of tone bursts (lower trace).

Frequency selectivity of the cochlea

In recent years there has been some controversy concerning the frequency selectivity of the cochlea. The broad-band tuning curves of the cochlear partition were obtained by von Békésy (1944) by vibrating the stapes and observing the motion of the partition under stroboscopic illumination. Tasaki (1954) employed microelectrodes to obtain the corresponding electrical tuning curves for the cochlea nerve of the guinea pig. The curves had a similar bandwidth to those obtained by von Békésy, leading to the conclusion that these curves represented the imput to the central nervous system (Whitfield, 1967). More recent work by Kiang *et al.* (1965, 1967), de Boer (1969) and Evans (1971) indicated that tuning curves could be obtained in cats which were very much sharper than the mechanical tuning curves obtained by von Békésy.

A new method of obtaining mechanical tuning curves employing the Mössbauer effect was devised by Johnstone (Johnstone and Boyle, 1967; Johnstone *et al.*, 1970). He employed this technique to obtain the frequency response at the basal end of the guinea-pig cochlea, and obtained results similar to those of von Békésy. Evans (1970, 1972) made new measurements on single units in the cochlea nerve of the guinea pig which indicated that these units could be as sharply tuned as those of the cat. As a result it was shown that there was a discrepancy of an order of magnitude in the sharpness of the mechanical and electrical tuning curves in animals of the same species.

Wilson and Johnstone (1972) employed a different technique to measure the mechanical tuning curves of the guinea-pig basilar membrane. They used a capacitive probe, developed by Wilson (1973), with a tip of only 0.15 mm diameter. They report results which are similar to those of Johnstone *et al.* (1970). In addition they found that basilar membrane displacement is proportional to sound pressure level up to 110-dB SPL. Rhode (1971) has used the Mössbauer technique to investigate basilar membrane motion in squirrel monkeys. Under the same conditions he obtained broad tuning curves similar to those of Johnstone and Wilson. Contrary to Wilson's finding, however, he reports non-linearities with sound pressure levels as low as 70-dB SPL.

Evans (1972) has developed a semi-automatic technique for obtaining neural tuning curves. Once a unit has been found, an on-line computer program sweeps the frequency and amplitude of the stimulus through the ranges of the unit, and records the resultant spike count. A plot similar to that shown in Fig. 2.9 is obtained. He has used this method to investigate the effects of various kinds of damage on neural tuning curves. He finds that with the cochlea opened (which is necessary with the Mössbauer technique) or with the perilymph drained from the scala tympani (which is necessary with the capacitive probe technique) sharp neural tuning curves are still obtained (Evans and Wilson, 1973).

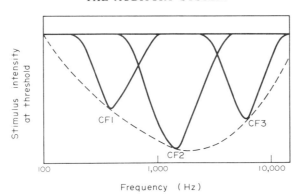

Fig. 2.9. Hypothetical curves showing the responsiveness of three neurones. The minimum stimulus intensity which causes the neurone to fire is plotted against stimulus frequency. The characteristic frequency (CF) of each neurone is shown.

In order to explain the enhanced sharpness of the neural curves, the existence of a "second filter" has been suggested. It is supposed to be located in the cochlea functionally between the basilar membrane and the cochlear nerve; that is somewhere in the region of the hair cells. Evans (1974) has shown that various chemical agents eliminate the action of this filter, giving neural tuning curves whose shapes approximate those of the mechanical tuning curves.

Units of the lower auditory system

At the level of the cochlear nerve most neurones are spontaneously active; they produce spike discharges in the absence of sound stimuli. Their discharge is accelerated by a tone lying within the "tuning curve" area bordering the characteristic frequency of each neurone. The response continues for the duration of the tone, followed by a reduction in the level of spontaneous activity when the tone is turned off. The discharge rate is generally a monotonic function of tone intensity, but the dynamic response is limited to about 40 dB above the threshold of firing. For low-frequency tones (below 3 to 4 kHz) individual spike responses are time locked to cycles of the stimulus (Rose *et al.*, 1968). This pattern of activity is transmitted to the brain stem in a highly ordered fashion in terms of frequency: the neurones of the cochlear nucleus being ordered in terms of their characteristic frequencies. This tonotopic organization is preserved in the superior olivary complex (Tsuchitani and Boudreau, 1966) and in the inferior colliculus (Rose *et al.*, 1963). However, it has not been found in the medial geniculate body, and is not present in the auditory cortex (Evans, 1968).

In the cochlear nucleus the auditory system divides into two paths. The ventral pathway transmits the pattern of activity relatively unchanged to the superior olivary complex. The dorsal pathway, however, translates the excitatory frequency response regions of the cochlear nerve into inhibitory response areas (Evans and Nelson, 1973). Thus the monotonic relationship with the input is lost. The dorsal and ventral pathways converge in the lateral lemnisci to project to the higher levels of the system. It is not surprising, therefore, that the responses at the inferior colliculi should show greater variety and complexity.

Nelson *et al.* (1966) have found a number of neurones in the inferior colliculi of cats which exhibited some selectivity to tones whose amplititudes were sinusoidally modulated. Some neurones responded only to amplitude-modulated stimuli. Many were sensitive to the direction of modulation. In these cases the nature and magnitude of the responses were critically dependent on the rate and depth of modulation. Vartanyan (1969) has confirmed these findings in rats.

Lateral suppression

So far only the behaviour of the auditory system in response to sinusoidal tones has been considered. Speech signals, however, are much more complex. They contain harmonics and noise bursts in an ever-changing succession. Even with animals most significant sounds, outside the laboratory, are much more complex than tones. The behaviour of the auditory system to more complicated sounds is, therefore, of great interest.

Sachs and Kiang (1967) have demonstrated that the presence of one tone can influence the response of a unit to a second tone. Their technique was to determine the characteristic frequency of a unit in the auditory nerve, then to supply a continuous tone at this frequency and measure the discharge rate in response to a varying tone in the tuning curve area. The results they obtained are shown in Fig. 2.10. In the centre

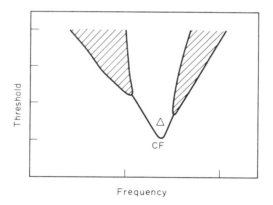

Fig. 2.10. Two-tone suppression. The responsiveness of the unit to a tone in the shaded region is reduced by the presence of a tone at the CF.

region they found that the second tone increased the discharge rate, whereas in regions to either side at higher and lower frequencies, the second tone suppressed the discharge rate. At greater differences from the characteristic frequency, the second tone had no effect.

Multiple-peak stimuli

There are relatively few other reports of systematic studies of the responses of neurones to stimuli composed of more than one frequency component. Wilson and Evans (1971) added a white noise to a delayed version of itself. This produces a stimulus whose spectrum is shown in Fig. 2.11. It consists of a multiple-peak stimulus,

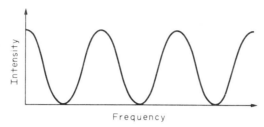

Fig. 2.11. Spectrum of comb-filtered noise formed by adding white noise to a delayed version of itself. The peak spacing can be varied with the delay.

the peaks being separated by a frequency equal to the reciprocal of the delay. This was used to examine the frequency resolving power of primary auditory neurones. At this level a straightforward spectral analysis appears to take place. The neurones respond as would be predicted on the basis that their pure tone frequency threshold characteristics represent linear filtering.

Units in the auditory cortex

In the auditory cortex there is a smaller proportion of units which respond to a steady tone with a continuous discharge. Many units are inhibited by the presence of tones from discharging spikes. Some units respond with a burst of spikes only when the unit is turned on ("on" response), others when the tone is turned off ("off" response), and some with one burst at the beginning of the tone and another at the end ("on–off" response). The distribution of units found in the auditory cortex of cat by Evans and Whitfield (1964) is given in Table 2.1.

Many of the neurones at cortical level respond only to very complex sounds such as clicks or random noise. In fact these kinds of stimuli are the most effective in terms of the certainty of obtaining a response, whereas at the lower levels of the auditory system, such stimuli are only effective by virtue of their spectral energy content. Evans *et al.* (1970) have shown at this low level the response to noise stimuli can be predicted from their pure tone behaviour. Of particular interest to theories of speech recognition, are units in the cortex which respond only to sliding tones (frequency modulated tones) and not to steady tones. These were originally discovered by Bogdanski and Galambos (1960), but were studied in detail by Evans and Whitfield (1964). They found that these units were all sensitive to the direction, and to some extent the rate, of frequency change. Watanabe and Ohgushi (1968) have attempted to correlate the preferred direction and rate of frequency change with the vocalization of the cat. The vocalizations contain frequency changes which are slow in the downward direction but rapid in

Table 2.1. Classification of units in the primary auditory cortex of
cat (Evans and Whitfield, 1964)

Stimulus or response	Number of units	Percent
Total units	163	100
1. Sound	125	77
2. Visual stimulation	5	2.5
3. Sound and light	1	0.5
4. Unresponsive	32	20
Units responding to sounds	125	77
5. Tones	88	54
6. Clicks and "odd" sounds	34	21
7. Unclassified	3	2
Units responding to tones	88	54
8. Sustained excitation	40	24
9. Sustained inhibition	16	10
10. "On" response	10	6
11. "Off" response	9	6
12. "On–off" response	4	2.5
13. 9 and 10 or 12	1	0.5
14. Sliding tones only	6	4
15. Unclassified.	2	1

both upward and downward directions. Winter and Funkenstein (1973) have found a few units in the auditory cortex of squirrel monkeys which appear to respond only to specific monkey vocalizations and not to other sounds.

The responses of many neurones depend on the temporal patterning of the stimuli (Evans, 1968). Some units respond best to a frequently repeated stimulus; but most habituate, responding vigorously to the first few presentations of the stimulus, but rapidly ceasing to respond when the stimulus is repeated over and over again.

CHAPTER 3

Auditory Psychophysics

The ability of listeners to perceive and discriminate sounds is the subject of this chapter. The various mechanisms employed by the hearing system to analyse sounds have been described. Now the behaviour of the complete system will be explored. In the previous chapter most of the work described was based on experiments with the hearing systems of animals, but in this chapter the data were obtained from human listeners by presenting them with acoustic stimuli and recording their responses.

Threshold of hearing

The absolute sensitivity of the ear is measured as the smallest sound pressure which leads to the sensation of hearing. There are two methods by which this threshold of hearing can be measured: the closed-field method in which the sound source is placed tightly against the ear, and the open-field method with the source placed some distance away.

The first method is most convenient, especially for separate measurements of the right and left ears. It is, however, more liable to error than the open-field method because of the very small sound pressures which can be perceived. The open-field

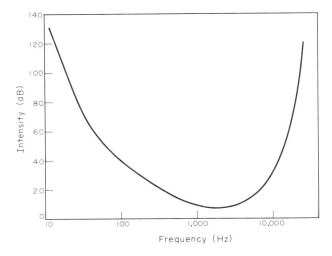

Fig. 3.1. Threshold of hearing as a function of frequency for a typical young adult.

23

method is more natural, but care has to be taken to avoid reflections. For this reason the measures should be made in an anechoic chamber.

The threshold of hearing depends on the frequency of the sound. The human ear is most sensitive between 1000 and 3000 Hz with the threshold rising for lower and higher frequencies. Figure 3.1 shows a typical threshold curve for a normal young listener. If the threshold at 1000 Hz is taken as a reference, the signal has to be increased a hundred times to reach the threshold at 100 Hz and 15,000 Hz, and a thousand times to reach the threshold at 18,000 Hz. The threshold for the loudest sounds which can be tolerated (the terminal threshold) does not vary appreciably with frequency. Discomfort occurs more or less uniformly when the sound pressure level reaches 40 dB above 1 dyne per cm². Sensation of tickle and pain occur when the pressure is raised by another 20 dB. The range of intensity between absolute and terminal thresholds for a 1000-Hz tone is thus about 140 dB.

Intensity discrimination

The smallest detectable change in the intensity of a tone is called the intensity difference limen (DL). This may be expressed as the absolute amount of change which is just noticeably different (ΔI), or as the relative change ($\Delta I / I$). It has been found that ΔI depends on the frequency and the intensity of the stimulating tone. One method of measuring ΔI was devised by Riesz (1928). He combined the signals from two oscillators which were mistuned by 3 Hz, and then raised the intensity of one of the signals until beats were heard. At 1000 Hz, he found that a tone with an intensity of 10 dB could just be discriminated from one of 14.6 dB, whereas one of 60 dB could be discriminated from one of 61 dB. In general, the difference limen decreases as the intensity of the tone is increased. The DL is least in the 1- to 3-kHz frequency region, and greater outside it.

Frequency thresholds

The frequency limits of hearing are generally considered to lie between 20 and 20,000 Hz. At moderate sound intensities (80 dB) the upper limit is often no higher than 18,000 Hz, but by increasing the intensity the upper limit can be extended. It cannot be increased indefinitely, however, because a practical limit is imposed by pain. The absolute intensity threshold coincides with the pain threshold at about 23,000 Hz, making this the practical upper limit of hearing. There may be a higher limit imposed by the failure of one or more mechanisms of the ear, but for obvious reasons little data are available. From single-unit and other studies, it is known that many animals have good hearing in the ultrasonic region. Below 20 Hz the time interval between energy peaks is too great for listeners to perceive a fused tonal quality. Nevertheless, down to about 10 Hz an auditory sensation known as 'flutter" occurs.

The frequency range of hearing is thus about 10 Hz to 23,000 Hz, but the range for which sounds have a definite pitch is limited to 20 Hz to 20,000 Hz.

Frequency discrimination

The frequency difference limen is a measure of the ability of a listener to detect a change in the frequency of a tone. The classical measurements were made by Shower and Biddulph (1931). Their technique was to present a tone of frequency f_1 for a short time, then to change the frequency sinusoidally to f_2, and then back to f_1. The frequency f_2 was adjusted until the listener just detected a difference. The difference limen Δf was then equal to $(f_1 - f_2)$. It was found that changing the frequency about twice a second gave the best results.

Frequency discrimination was at one time thought to be described by Weber's law, which stated that

$$\Delta f/f = \text{a constant.}$$

Shower and Biddulph showed that this holds approximately in the 500-Hz to 8000-Hz region, but not at lower frequencies. They also showed that Δf increases as the intensity of the tone is lowered.

Shower and Biddulph found that for a tone with an intensity of about 40 dB, Δf was about 3 Hz in the 125 Hz to 2000 Hz region, 12 Hz at 5000 Hz, and 30 Hz at 10,000 Hz. A more recent determination of the frequency DL has been made by Nordmark (1968). He presented two tone bursts, each with an intensity of 45 dB and with waveforms as shown in Fig. 3.2, to a listener. Each tone was 800 msec in duration separated by a silent

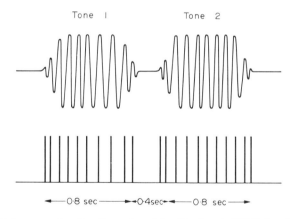

Fig. 3.2. Waveform of the acoustic stimuli employed by Nordmark (1968) for the determination of the frequency DL.

400-msec interval. The listener was instructed to adjust the frequency of the second tone until it sounded the same as the first. The experimenter recorded the setting, and then calculated the DL as the standard deviation of the final settings (the frequency of the second tone).

The results obtained by Nordmark showed that the frequency DL is somewhat smaller than given by Shower and Biddulph's results. When the frequency DL's were plotted on a log-log scale, they could be approximated by two straight lines. At 100 Hz the DL was about 0.2 Hz rising to about 1.5 Hz at 2000 Hz, and thence more steeply to about 30 Hz at 12,000 Hz.

Pitch

Pitch is the subjective attribute of a sound which corresponds to the physical attribute of frequency. Although the pitch of a pure tone is monotonically related to its frequency, a linear relationship does not hold. A pitch scale was established by Stevens and Volkmann (1940) by asking listeners to adjust the frequency of one tone so that its pitch was half as high as that of a second tone. This is known as the method of fractionation. The unit of pitch is the "mel". A tone with a frequency of 1000 Hz is defined as having a pitch of 1000 mels. The relationship between the pitch scale and the frequency scale for pure tones of 40-dB intensity is shown in Fig. 3.3.

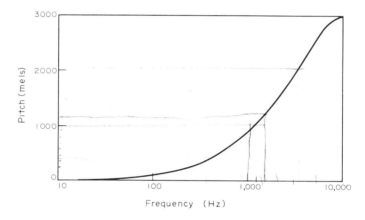

Fig. 3.3. Relationship between pitch and frequency as determined by the method of fractionation (Stevens and Volkmann, 1940).

A tone with a pitch of 500 mels sounds half as high as one with a pitch of 1000 mels. However, its frequency will be 400 Hz. Similarly a tone with a pitch of 2000 mels will sound twice as high as one with a pitch of 1000 mels, yet its frequency will be 3000 Hz rather than 2000 Hz.

It has been observed (Stevens, 1935) that the pitch of a tone depends upon its intensity. In general, the middle frequencies have relatively stable pitches, whereas tones of low frequencies have their pitches shifted downwards as the intensity is increased, and tones of high frequencies have their pitches shifted upwards.

The onset of a pure tone is not accompanied instantaneously by a sensation of pitch. It usually takes up to a quarter of a second before a stable pitch is heard, though the time required depends on the frequency (Turnbull, 1944). In general it appears that a critical duration must elapse before a stable pitch is heard. Below 1000 Hz the critical duration is a fixed number of cycles (6 ± 3), whereas above 1000 Hz the critical duration is a fixed interval of time (about 10 msec).

Loudness

Just as pitch is the subjective correlate of frequency, loudness is the subjective correlate of intensity. Again, loudness is a monotonic, but not a linear, function of intensity. Using the method of fractionation the form of the relationship has been derived by Churcher (1935) and by Fletcher (1938). The shape of the curve is shown in Fig. 3.4.

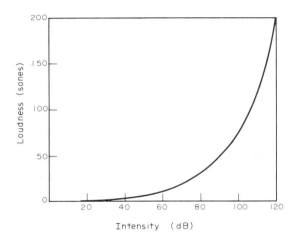

Fig. 3.4. Relationship between the loudness and intensity of a 1000-Hz tone (Sevens and Davis, 1938).

If the standard is a 1000-Hz tone with an intensity of 40 dB above the threshold of hearing, the unit of loudness is the "sone" (Stevens and Davis, 1938). Loudness depends to some extent on frequency, but the curve shown in Fig. 3.4 is approximately correct for frequencies between 500 Hz and 4000 Hz.

In order to compare tones of different frequencies, another unit, the "phon", is used. The loudness of any tone in phons is defined as equal to the intensity in decibels of a 1000-Hz tone judged to be of equal loudness.

For short tones, loudness depends on duration. For durations of less than about 200 msec, the intensity has to be increased in order to obtain the same subjective loudness (Lifshitz, 1933; Garner and Miller, 1944; Munson, 1947; Stevens, 1973). Typically the intensity of a tone of 10-msec duration must be about 10 dB greater than that of a tone of 200 msec (or longer) duration, in order to give the same sensation of loudness.

Critical bands

When a weak tone is heard in the presence of an adjacent tone, the threshold for hearing the first tone is raised. This phenomenon is known as "masking". Fletcher and Munson (1937) found that the threshold is raised only when the tones are close to each other in frequency. If they are more than a critical distance apart, the second tone has no effect on the threshold for hearing the first tone. These experiments have led to the concept of the "critical band". Signals within the critical band influence the perception of other signals within the critical band, but not those outside.

Critical bands were measured throughout the frequency range of hearing by listening to tones mixed with bandlimited noise. The tone was set at the centre frequency of the band of noise (Fig. 3.5). As the bandwidth of the noise was increased, the intensity at which the tone was just perceived also had to be increased until the bandwidth of the noise was equal to the critical band. Thereafter, the intensity for hearing the tone remained constant. It was found that critical bandwidth increases as the centre frequency is raised. The critical bandwidth for a centre frequency of 200 Hz was found to be about 100 Hz, and for 5000 Hz about 1000 Hz.

It will be remembered (Chapter 2) that the point of maximum vibration moves along the basilar membrane as the frequency of excitation is increased. If this relationship is used to translate critical bandwidths into distance along the basilar membrane, it will be found that a critical bandwidth is equivalent to a distance of approximately 1.2 mm for all frequencies in the range 200 Hz to 16,000 Hz. Above and below this range, the bandwidths correspond to distances greater than 1.2 mm.

It is probable that the physiological origin of the critical band phenomenon is the spread of hair cells connected to a single neurone in the cochlear nerve. Two tones within the same critical band will stimulate some of the same neurones, and so will interfere with the perception of each other; whereas tones in different critical bands will stimulate different sets of neurones and will be transmitted to the higher parts of the auditory system independently.

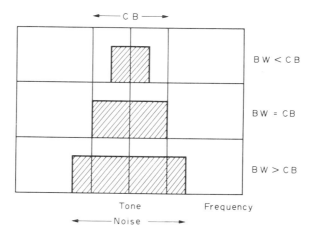

Fig. 3.5. Critical bands. The threshold for hearing the tone increases until the bandwidth of the noise equals the critical band, and thereafter remains constant.

Perception of duration

The ability of human listeners to discriminate between tones of different durations has been measured by Creelman (1962) and Abel (1972a). The method used by Abel was to present listeners with two tones differing only in duration, and to ask them to decide which was the longer. It was found that the difference in duration of the tones (ΔT) with which this task could be performed correctly 75 per cent of the time depended on the overall length of the tones (T). The results could be approximated by a straight line on a log-log plot. ΔT is about 0.5 msec for tones of 0.5-msec duration, and about 50 msec for tones of 500 msec duration. In the region of interest in speech perception, 10 to 100 msec, the measured values of ΔT were 2 to 5 msec. Similar results were obtained with noise bursts having bandwidths in the range 200 to 3500 Hz as with 1000-Hz tones.

Abel (1972b) has also measured the accuracy with which silent gaps of various durations can be discriminated. ΔT was found to be about 2 msec for 1-msec gaps, and 100 msec for 500-msec gaps. In the region 10 to 100 msec, ΔT was approximately 20 msec. These values were reduced slightly when the intensity of the sounds which marked the beginning and end of the silent gaps were increased from 70 to 85 dB. Similar experiments have been performed by Fujisaki et al. (1975). They found a similar value for the accuracy of discriminating gaps of 100 msec between tones, 21 msec, but slightly lower accuracies for discriminating the durations of 500-Hz tones, 8 msec for 50-msec tones to 23 msec for 300-msec tones. Similarly with white noise bursts of 100 msec, an accuracy of about 9 msec was found.

Fatigue

When a listener hears a sound for a relatively long period its loudness appears to decrease. This is accompanied by a measurable increase in the threshold of hearing, and is known as "fatigue". In the experiments of Causse and Chavasse (1947), listeners heard a pure tone of a certain duration, then they adjusted a test tone until it was just perceived. With a 1000-Hz tone of 40-dB intensity it was found that the threshold shifted about 1 dB for every 10 sec of exposure in the range 10 to 40 sec. For a tone of 10-dB intensity, the shift was about half as great.

Causse and Chavasse found similar shifts for all tones with frequencies in the region of 1000 Hz to 10,000 Hz. Below 500 Hz, however, no threshold shift was found with a tone of 40-dB intensity.

The reduction in loudness of a tone can be measured by a binaural method. One ear is exposed to sound for a certain duration, then a test tone is applied to the other ear and its intensity is adjusted until its loudness matches that of the original tone. It has been found that loudness reduces exponentially for about 2 min from the time the tone is turned on, then it becomes stable for longer periods of exposure.

Exposure to noise also causes a reduction in loudness. Carterette (1956) has shown that if intensity and duration are held constant, loudness decreases with increase in the bandwidth of the noise. There is more fatiguing when the energy is spread out across the spectrum.

Recovery from fatigue follows an exponential course (Rawnsley and Harris, 1952; Thwing, 1955). When the exposure is to sounds whose intensities are insufficient to cause injury, normal threshold and loudness sensitivity are restored within a minute of the cessation of the stimulus sound. With very intense, prolonged stimulation, recovery takes several hours, and in the extreme case a permanent threshold shift may occur.

Masking

The situation in which masking occurs has been mentioned briefly in the discussion of critical bands. When one tone (the maskee) is heard in the presence of a second tone (the masker), the threshold for hearing the maskee is raised. Wengel and Lane (1924) showed that for tones of moderate intensity (44 dB) the greatest elevation in threshold occurred when the maskee was within the critical bandwidth of the masker (Fig. 3.6).

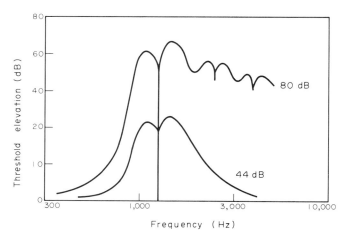

Fig. 3.6. Elevation of threshold as a function of frequency for 1200-Hz masking tones of 44 and 80 dB (Wengel and Lane, 1924).

For higher intensity tones (80 dB), however, the threshold was elevated for all frequencies above the frequency of the masker. This was probably caused by aural harmonics which were of sufficient intensity to act as maskers.

It is possible to mask tones applied to one ear by tones applied to the contralateral ear, but the masking effects are greatly reduced compared with ipsilateral masking. This effect probably depends on bone conduction across the head, but the possibility of central nervous interference has not been entirely ruled out.

Pulsation thresholds

A new paradigm for studying masking has recently been introduced by Houtgast (1972). The masker is gated periodically, 125 msec on and 125 msec off, and the test tone is presented during the silent intervals. As the intensity of the test tone is raised the listener first hears just the masker pulses, then a continuous tone, and finally a pulsating tone. The task of the listener is to adjust the level of the test tone to the borderline between the continuous and pulsating tones. It is argued that this "pulsation threshold" might be considered as an indication of the apparent level of the masker's auditory spectrum in the region of the test tone.

Houtgast employed a masker consisting of two tones, a weak tone (fixed at 1000 Hz, 40 dB) and a strong tone of variable frequency and intensity. The test tone had a frequency of 1000 Hz, and its intensity was controlled by the listener. The values of the

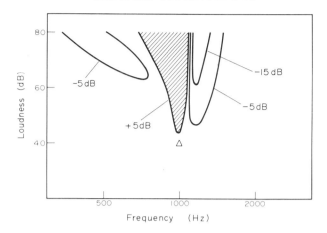

Fig. 3.7. Pulsation thresholds. The threshold for hearing a test tone centred at the weak tone (triangle) in the
presence of a variable strong tone is shown by the contours (Houtgast, 1973).

pulsation thresholds that were obtained are shown in Fig. 3.7. When the two tones of
the masker had nearly the same frequency as each other and the test tone (1000 Hz), the
intensity of the test tone must be raised, as expected. When the strong tone is different
from the weak tone, however, the intensity of the test tone must be reduced for the
pulsation threshold.

The similarity between the results of this experiment and the two-tone suppression
in neurones of the auditory nerve (Sachs and Kiang, 1968) has been noted. There is as
yet, however, no reason to suppose that these results reflect neural activity at such a
peripheral place in the auditory system.

Theories of hearing

In 1863 Helmholtz published his "resonance" theory of hearing. The basilar
membrane was considered to be a series of independently tuned resonators. These
resonators performed a Fourier analysis and transmitted the intensity of each frequency component to the brain as the strength of the corresponding nerve discharges.
Anatomical evidence, however, showed the basilar membrane to be a continuous
structure, rather than a set of discrete elements. This led Rutherford in 1886 to propose
a theory of hearing in which the frequency components of the stimulus were
transmitted to the brain by synchronous neural discharges. These two theories have
continued in various forms and are now known as the "place" and "volley" theories.
The travelling wave theory of von Békésy (1928) provides the mechanism for the place
theory. The oscillatory motion of the stapes causes sudden fluid pressure changes,
forcing a wave to travel along the basilar membrane. The place of maximum amplitude
varies with the frequency of the acoustic stimulus.

Some experiments by Schouten (1938, 1940) cast doubt on the place theory as the
only mechanism of hearing. He showed that if two tones, f_1 and f_2, are listened to
simultaneously, a pitch corresponding to a frequency of f_2-f_1 is also heard. He termed
this the "residue" pitch. If the place theory were correct, there should be peaks in the

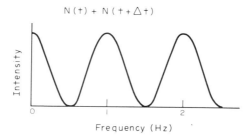

Fig. 3.8. Spectrum of comb-filtered noise. A noise signal, $N(t)$, is added to a delayed version of itself, $N(t + \Delta t)$, $\Delta t = 1$ msec (Wilson, 1967).

amplitude of the travelling wave only at f_1 and f_2 and not at $f_2 - f_1$ (except in the case of non-linear distortion, and Schouten was careful to exclude this), so no such pitch should be heard. In order to explain his observations, Schouten suggested that there were neural discharges in synchrony with the amplitude maxima of the combined f_1 and f_2 wave. These maxima occur at a period corresponding to $f_2 - f_1$. Pitches corresponding to other frequencies, such as $2f_1 - f_2$, have since been reported.

This "volley" theory of hearing, where the neurones discharge in synchrony with some feature of the acoustic wave has some physiological evidence in favour of it, but at higher frequencies the time intervals involved are too brief for the neurones to fire and recover in time to fire again. For this reason Wever (1949) combined the place and volley theories. He considered that the principle of the volley theory operates from 20 to 400 Hz. Between 400 Hz and 5000 Hz a modified volley principle operates in which neurones fire on every second, and then third, peak as the frequency is increased.

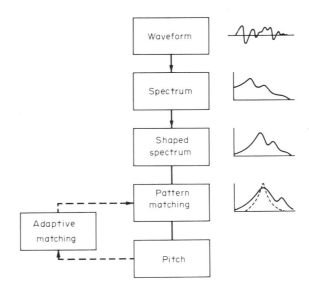

Fig. 3.9. A pattern recognition theory of pitch perception.

Above 5000 Hz the place principle is evoked. Loudness is supposed to be coded by the number of neurones which discharge.

It is difficult to devise experiments which will discriminate between the place and volley theories as, according to Fourier, frequency and time are equivalent modes of description of a signal. A stimulus employed by Wilson (1967), however, goes some way towards this. A white noise is added to a delayed version of itself, and the result is a signal whose spectrum contains peaks and troughs separated by a frequency equal to the reciprocal of the delay (Fig. 3.8). On the place theory this signal should give rise to a pitch which depends on this delay. As the signal is composed of noise there is no periodically repeated waveform, so on the volley theory no steady pitch should be heard. The pitch which is in fact elicited by this stimulus is approximately that predicted by the place theory.

In order to combine this result with the "residue" phenomenon, Wilson (1973) has suggested a "pattern recognition" theory. A mechanism matches a set of stored patterns against the spectrum of the incoming signal in the dominant region of the spectrum and the pitch which is heard is that of the pattern which matches the best. For example, if the patterns consist of series of harmonics of tones, a pattern can be found with harmonics spaced at f_2-f_1, which will match tones at f_1 and f_2, and similarly a pattern can be found which will match the peaks of the noise-plus-delayed-noise stimulus (Fig. 3.9).

CHAPTER 4

Speech Analysis

The sounds of speech form a very small subset of the acoustic signals which the auditory system is capable of analysing. In this chapter the various techniques of analysing speech sounds will be discussed. These range from the simple display of the speech waveform, through spectrum analysis (which has special relevance due to its functional similarities with the action of the cochlea), to statistical analysis of the occurrence of the sounds of speech in language.

Speech waveforms

Voiced sounds are produced by phonation, as described in Chapter 1. Pulses of air from the larynx excite the natural resonances of the vocal tract, and the sound radiates from the lips (Fig. 4.1). The waveforms of a set of naturally produced vowels are shown

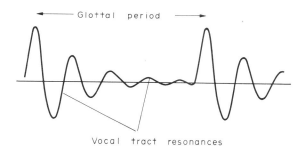

Fig. 4.1. An idealized speech waveform.

in Fig. 4.2. With the front vowels /i,ɪ,ɛ,æ/ the frequencies of the lowest two resonances are far apart, and the ripples of the wave which are due to these can readily be separated. With the back vowels /u,ʊ,ɔ,ɒ,ɑ/ the resonances are closer in frequency, and consequently the corresponding ripples are more difficult to discriminate.

Speech waveform analysis is useful for studying larynx vibrations as the start of each glottal cycle can usually be clearly seen. The period from the start of one cycle to the start of the next normally varies slightly even when an attempt is made to keep the pitch of the vowel constant. In normal conversational speech, where pitch is used to indicate stressed syllables and grammatical constructions, the glottal period is constantly changing. It is sometimes desirable to examine the glottal waveform before it is modified by the resonances of the vocal tract. One way to do this is by means of a throat

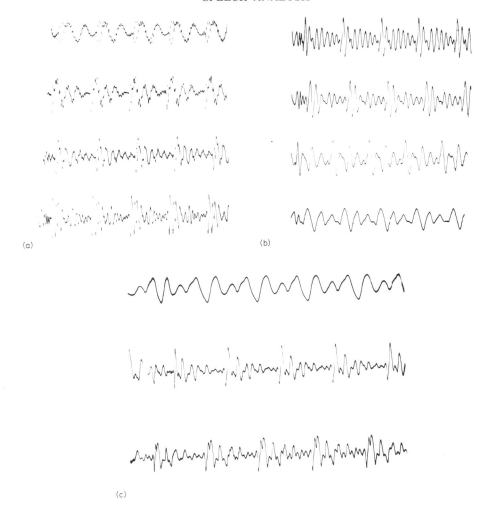

Fig. 4.2. Waveforms of the vowels (a) /i,ɪ,ɛ,æ/, (b) /ɑ,ɒ,ɔ,ʊ/, and (c) /u,ʌ,ɜ/.

microphone, but this does pick up some of the vocal tract vibrations. A more successful method is to employ the laryngograph, a modern form of which has recently been produced by Fourcin and Abberton (1971), developed from the original method of Fabre (1959). Electrodes are placed on the outside of the throat either side of the larynx. A high-frequency signal is passed between them. As the glottis opens and closes the impedance between the electrodes changes, and this is reflected in the current which flows. A larynx waveform obtained by this method is shown in Fig. 4.3.

Although waveform analysis offers certain advantages, it also presents serious drawbacks. Firstly, the resonances of the vocal tract are not easily separable, and secondly, the time scale is such that it is difficult to study more than a few successive cycles. The average frequency of vibration of the male larynx is about 120 Hz. A typical

Fig. 4.3. Typical glottal waveform as measured by laryngograph.

glottal period is thus about 8 msec in duration. A typical sentence takes perhaps 2 sec to utter. If each period is displayed in less than a centimetre the oscillations will be difficult to see, so the sentence could not usefully be displayed in less than 2.5 metres.

Spectrum analysis

These difficulties can be virtually eliminated if the waveform is transformed into its spectrum, and the spectrum is displayed. The Fourier transform of a waveform $f(t)$ is given by

$$F(\omega) = \int_{-\infty}^{\infty} f(t)\, e^{-j\omega t}\, dt.$$

The function $f(t)$ is not known for speech for all time, so this operation cannot be carried out directly.

What is required for speech analysis is a "running" spectrum, the spectrum over a short period of time. This can be obtained by viewing the waveform through a window, or weighting function $h(t)$. A Fourier transformable signal results if $h(t)$ is taken as the response of a low-pass filter. The operation is

$$F(\omega, t) = \int_{-\infty}^{t} f(\lambda) h(t - \lambda)\, e^{-j\omega\lambda}\, d\lambda$$

where λ is a dummy integration variable.

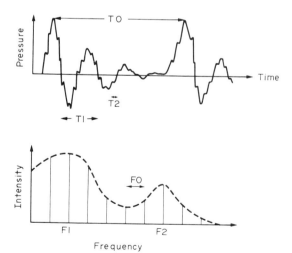

Fig. 4.4. Relationship between speech waveform and spectrum (F0 = 1/T0 is the fundamental frequency, F1 = /T1 is the first formant frequency, and F2 = /T2 is the second formant frequency).

It can be shown (Flanagan, 1965, pp. 120–4) that a practical method of performing this operation is to employ a band-pass filter, followed by a rectifier and low-pass filter as shown in Fig. 4.4. A set of band-pass filters arranged in parallel give a running spectrum of the input waveform.

According to the uncertainty relationship of Gabor (1946):

$$\Delta f \cdot \Delta t \geqslant \tfrac{1}{2}$$

where Δf is the frequency resolution and Δt is the time resolution. Thus if the widths of the band-pass filters are narrow so that Δf is small, the signal will not be well resolved in time. If the harmonics of the male voice are to be resolved, Δf should be less than 100 Hz. If Δf is set at 50 Hz, then Δt will be 20 msec. The period of each glottal cycle will be about 8 msec, so each glottal period will not be resolved. On the other hand, for Δt to be 5 msec so that each glottal period is resolved, Δf must be set at 200 Hz and the harmonics will not be resolved. In certain instances one of these conditions is required, and in others the other condition will be required, so it is desirable to have two banks of analysing filters.

Sound spectrograph

An alternative to a bank of band-pass filters is to employ a single analysing filter but to replay the speech many times and to change the pass-band for each repetition. This forms the basis of the sound spectrograph, or sonagraph (Koenig *et al.*, 1946; Potter *et al.*, 1947). The speech to be analysed is recorded on a disc (Fig. 4.5). As the disc rotates,

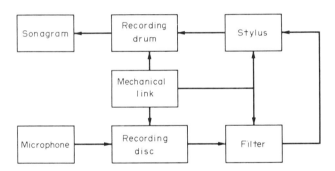

Fig. 4.5. Functional diagram of the sound spectograph.

the speech is replayed over and over again through the filter. The filter is initially set so that its centre frequency has a low value (about 100 Hz). The output from the filter is rectified and the resulting current passed from the stylus through the recording paper to a metal cylinder. The paper is blackened by this current.

As the disc rotates a screw is turned which causes the stylus to be moved up the paper. A potentiometer is also attached to this screw which effectively sweeps the centre frequency of the analysing filter through its range. The density of the trace on the paper is approximately proportional to the logarithm of the current which passes so that as the stylus sweeps across the paper on the rotating cylinder and the centre frequency of the band-pass filter is swept through its range, a frequency–intensity–time plot of the signal is formed on the paper. A typical sound spectrogram, or sonagram, of the sentence "Mechanisms of speech recognition" is shown in Fig. 4.6.

Most sonagraphs are fitted with two analysing filters, typically with bandwidths of 300 Hz and 45 Hz. The wide-band filter is employed when good time resolution is necessary. In the sonagram in the upper part of Fig. 4.6 the glottal pulses are resolved by using the wide-band filter. In the lower part of the figure the harmonics of the glottal pulses are resolved by using the narrow-band filter. A conventional sound spectrograph enables about 2.5 sec of speech to be recorded and analysed. The resulting sonagram is a plot about 10 cm by 30 cm. Thus a convenient analysis of a complete sentence can be carried out.

Another advantage of spectrum analysis over waveform analysis is that it enables the major resonances of the signal to be separated. These can be clearly seen in the upper part of Fig. 4.6. These concentrations of energy at the resonant frequencies are known as "formants". They are conventionally numbered in ascending order with increasing frequency. Thus the formant having the lowest frequency is called "formant one", the next "formant two", etc.

The differences between voiced sounds and fricative sounds can clearly be seen in a wide-band sonagram. Thus voiced sounds are shown by vertical striations, each stripe representing the energy from a single glottal pulse. The fricative sounds, on the other hand, have no regular structure, and so appear as an irregular speckled pattern. One of the disadvantages of the sonagram is dynamic range of the blackening of the recording paper. The intensity range of speech is 50–60 dB, whereas that of the paper is about 12 dB. This smaller range can be compensated for to some extent by applying high-frequency pre-emphasis to the signal before analysis.

If the full dynamic range of the signal is to be investigated a device called a "sectioner" may be employed. This produces a conventional amplitude-frequency plot of the signal at a specific point in time. A cam on the rotating cylinder is set to the point at which the analysis is to be made. Each time the cylinder rotates, this triggers a circuit which causes a line to be drawn on the recording paper whose length is proportional to the logarithm of the intensity of the signal in the analysing filter. The frequency of the filter and the position of the stylus sweep through their ranges as before. The result is a "section" through the sonagram as shown in Fig. 4.7. An alternative method of displaying a sound spectrogram, which maintains the time structure of the utterance and also shows the true dynamic range of intensities, is to plot the amplitude by means of a series of contour lines (Kersta, 1948).

Vowel sounds

The vowel sounds appear on sonagrams as relatively intense patterns. As the articulators are more or less steady, the resonances remain constant for a short while, and appear as formants parallel to the time axis.

Sonagrams of some of the vowels of English spoken by male and female voices are shown in Fig. 4.8. For an /i/ sound the first formant is low and the second is high. For a /u/ sound, the frequency of the first formant is similar to that of an /i/ sound, but the second formant is much lower. For an /ɑ/ sound the first formant is high, but the second

Fig. 4.6. Sonagrams of the phrase "Mechanisms of speech recognition". Wide-band analysis above, and narrow-band below.

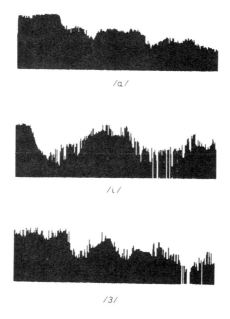

Fig. 4.7. Sections of sonagrams of the vowels /ɑ,i,ɜ/.

formant is low. Consequently the formants merge into a single, broad formant which is difficult to separate into its component parts. It will be seen that the open–close dimension of the articulatory domain corresponds approximately to the frequency of the first formant. The vowels /i/ and /u/ which are produced with a narrow (close) vocal tract have low first formant frequencies, whereas /ɑ/ and /æ/, produced with a wide (open) vocal tract, have relatively high first formant frequencies. In a similar way the frequency of the second formant corresponds to the front–back dimension of the articulatory domain. The front vowels /i,ɪ,ɛ,æ/ have higher second formant frequencies than the back vowels /u,ɔ,ɑ/. If the frequency of the first formant is plotted against the frequency of the second formant (Fig. 4.9), a diagram results which is similar to the vowel quadrilateral (Jones, 1949) used by phoneticians for describing how vowels should be pronounced relative to the "cardinal" vowels.

It will be noticed that the vowels produced by the female speaker do not have the same formant frequencies as those produced by the male speaker (Fig. 4.8). This is because the vocal tract of the female is shorter than that of the male. Vowels produced by children have even higher formants than those produced by women (Peterson and Barney, 1952). The position of each vowel produced by a particular speaker, however, is always the same relative to the other vowels produced by that individual when plotted as the frequency of formant two against formant one.

The durations of vowels in syllables have been measured by Peterson and Lehiste (1960). The vowels were spoken in syllables in a constant reference frame so that the effects of stress and tempo would be the same in every case. The intrinsic durations of some American vowels are shown in Table 4.1. The vowels /i,æ,ɑ,ɔ,u/ may be classed as "long" vowels, and /ɪ,ɛ,ʊ,ə/ as short. Peterson and Lehiste found that the preceding

Fig. 4.8. Sonagrams of the vowels /i,ɔ,æ,u,ɑ/. Male voice above, and female voice below.

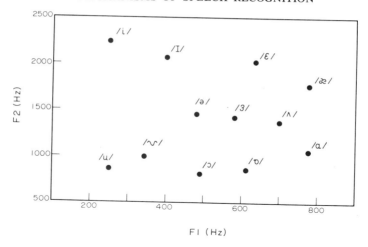

Fig. 4.9. Frequency of the second formant versus frequency of first formant for the vowels of English spoken by a typical male speaker.

consonant had negligible effect on the duration of the vowel, but the effect of the following consonant was considerable. The average durations of short and long vowels followed by various consonants are shown in Table 4.2. In every case the vowels were longer before a voiced consonant than before its voiceless counterpart. Plosives were preceded by the shortest vowels, nasals had approximately the same influence as voiced plosives, and voiced fricatives were preceded by the longest vowels.

Diphthongs

It was mentioned in Chapter 1 that diphthongs are sequences of two vowels spoken so that the second immediately follows the first. Consequently sonagrams of diphthongs are similar to those of pairs of vowels but with gradual transitions of the formants between the extremes (Fig. 4.10). The durations of diphthongs have been measured by Peterson and Lehiste (1960) and their results are shown in Table 4.3. The

Table 4.1. Intrinsic durations of vowels in American English (Peterson and Lehiste, 1959)

Vowel	Average duration (msec)
i	240
ɪ	180
ɛ	200
æ	330
ɑ	260
ɔ	310
ʋ	200
u	260
ə	230

Table 4.2. Durations of vowels as a function of the following consonant (Peterson and Lehiste, 1959)

Following consonant	Duration of short vowel (msec)	Duration of long vowel (msec)
p	138	188
b	203	307
t	147	210
d	206	318
k	145	200
g	243	314
m	220	313
n	216	322
ŋ	218	350
f	192	261
v	231	374
θ	208	265
ð	260	381
s	199	269
z	262	390
ʃ	212	278
ʒ	—	410
r	226	296
l	218	293
tʃ	145	198
dʒ	191	300

duration of each diphthong is somewhat less than the sum of the durations of its constituent vowels. During the articulation of a diphthong the intensity of the formants increases for a while, then decreases so that its final intensity is less than it was initially (Holbrook and Fairbanks, 1962). The effect of neighbouring consonants on the durations of diphthongs is similar to their effect on "long" vowels. Initial consonants have negligible effect, whereas final consonants influence duration as shown in Table 4.2.

Semivowels

The semivowels, being voiced sounds produced by movements of the articulators from one vowel configuration to another, produce similar sonagrams to the diphthongs (Fig. 4.11). The movements, however, are somewhat more rapid so the transitions are shorter (50–100 msec). In addition, the steady-state part of the first element is

Table 4.3. Intrinsic durations of diphthongs in American English (Peterson and Lehiste, 1959)

Diphthong	Duration (msec)
εi	270
əʊ	220
aʊ	300
ɑi	350
ɔi	370

exceedingly brief, except in emphatic speech. In the articulation of /w/ a configuration similar to that used to produce a /u/ is employed but this is held for only 10–20 msec. In a sonagram this shows up with the transitions beginning at the very start of the phoneme.

It will be seen from Fig. 4.11 that the initial frequencies of the formants of /j/ are very similar to the steady-state formant frequencies of /i/, those of /w/ are similar to those of /u/, and those of /r/ and /l/ are near to a more central vowel such as /ʌ/. The initial frequency of the third formant of /r/ is very low, so that a rapidly rising formant is characteristic of this phoneme when it occurs in front of a vowel.

Nasals

The sonagrams of nasals (Fig. 4.12) are similar to the vowels except that, because the sound is emitted via the nasal tract, which is longer than the oral tract, the pattern is dominated by a strong low-frequency first formant. The closed oral tract constitutes an extra resonator, and consequently the spectrum may contain zeros as well as poles.

Fujimura (1962) has analysed nasal consonants and finds considerable variability from one sample to another, depending on the individual nasal consonant and its context, and on the speaker. The common feature, besides a first formant with a frequency of about 300 Hz, is a high density of formants in the middle-frequency range between 800 Hz and 2300 Hz. There is a consistent lack of energy around 600 Hz which may be influenced by an anti-formant (zero) in the case of /m/. The velum, which is used to close the nasal tract when non-nasalized sounds are produced, can be moved quite rapidly. This gives rise to the rather abrupt boundary between nasal and vowel sounds which can be seen in the sonagrams.

Fricatives

Fricatives are produced by a narrow constriction in the vocal tract giving rise to turbulent flow of the air stream, rather than by periodic vibrations of the larynx. Consequently the vertical striations on the sonagrams of voiced sounds are absent. Instead there appears a more random pattern (Fig. 4.13). The voiceless fricatives are produced entirely by this method. The main difference between the patterns produced by them is the frequency region where the energy is concentrated and the intensity of the energy. According to Strevens (1960), the sounds fall into three groups: front, mid and back, corresponding to the regions of the vocal tract where they are produced. Sounds in the front group, /f/ and /θ/, have a wide distribution of energy with little patterning of peaks. Their relative intensity is low. Sounds in the mid group, /s/ and /ʃ/, have a concentrated spectrum with the main region of energy at a higher frequency than the other groups. The lowest frequency in /s/ is above 3500 Hz, whereas in /ʃ/ it lies between 1600 Hz and 2500 Hz. The relative energy of this group is high. The back group, which is represented in English by /h/, have a medium spread of energy exhibiting formant-like peaks. The relative energy is intermediate between the other groups. When /h/ is produced the vocal tract tends to assume the appropriate shape for the vowel following the /h/. Consequently the peaks of the spectrum are very variable depending on the context.

The voiced fricatives have mixed excitation: a mixture of periodic pulses from the larynx and random excitation from a constriction somewhere in the vocal tract. This shows in their sonagrams as vertical stripes in the low-frequency region of the spectrum and a random pattern in the upper region (Fig. 4.14). In general the concentration of fricative energy for each voiced fricative occurs in about the same frequency region as that of its voiceless counterpart, but the low-frequency, periodic energy is superimposed. The voiced fricatives have shorter durations than their voiceless equivalents.

Stop consonants

The stop consonants are produced by closure of the vocal tract at some point, allowing the pressure to build up, followed by the release. The sonagrams of stop consonants reflect this sequence of events (Fig. 4.15). During closure there is no energy in any part of the spectrum, and this is shown by a lack of blackening in the sonagram. The release is an impulsive excitation, generating energy at all frequencies. Immediately after the release, when the articulators involved in the closure are still close together, there may be turbulent flow with consequent fricative excitation. Once the larynx begins vibrating, the familiar vertical striations will appear on the sonagram. As the articulators will still be moving, formant transitions will be shown. An analysis of the acoustic properties of stop consonants has been made by Halle *et al.* (1957). With voiced stops, /b,d,g/, the larynx begins vibrating at or before the instant of release. (If it begins before, stripes can sometimes be seen during the "silent interval", prior to release. This is sometimes called the "voice bar".) In this case the formant transitions will be apparent. As the vocal tract is "close" for the period of closure, there is a rising first formant for each stop consonant. The transitions of the other formants depend upon the place of closure. For a /b/ the second formant normally rises, but for /d/ and /g/ the transitions depend on the following vowel. In voiceless stops, /p,t,k/, there is a delay of about 50 msec before the larynx begins vibrating. By this time the transitions are often completed, so the frequency of the concentration of energy in the burst must be used to distinguish between them. If the energy is in the low-frequency region the consonant is usually a /p/. If it is just above the second formant frequency, it is usually a /k/. Above 3000 Hz, the stop is normally a /t/. The spectrum of the noise does, however, vary considerably with the vowel which follows the consonant.

Affricates

Affricates are formed by a combination of stops and fricatives, and their sonagrams reflect this (Fig. 4.16). The voiced affricate /dʒ/, has most of the attributes of a voiced stop except there is some mixed excitation for a while. Similarly, /tʃ/ has the properties of a voiceless stop, but the fricative excitation continues for a longer than in a normal plosive. The durations of the affricates are less than the sum of the stops and fricatives of which they are composed.

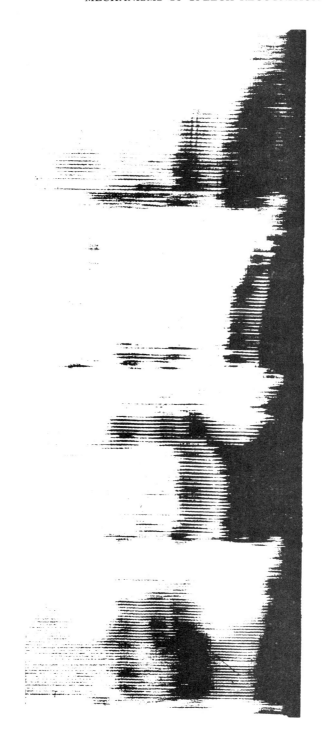

Fig. 4.10. Sonagrams of the diphthongs /ɛɪ/, /ʌɪ/, /ɑʊ/, /ʌe/.

Fig. 4.11. Sonagrams of the glides /w,r,l,j/.

Fig. 4.12. Sonagrams of the nasals /m,n/.

Fig. 4.13. Sonagrams of the voiceless fricatives /s,ʃ,f,θ/.

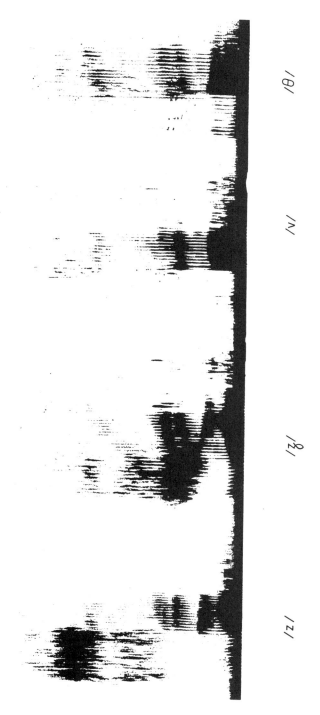

Fig. 4.14. Sonagrams of the voiced fricatives /z, ʒ, v, ð/.

Co-articulation

Analysis of speech into its frequency components has been shown to provide patterns of formant changes which reflect the articulatory pattern guestures which produce the sounds. When spoken in isolation these patterns may be sufficiently distinctive for the phoneme or syllable to be identified. Such an analysis may give the impression that speech is easily segmented into a string of phonemes and treated as such, in the same way that printed text may be treated as a string of letters. The statistical analyses which follow may reinforce this impression.

It must be remembered, however that the gestures of the articulators follow each other with extreme rapidity, and because of the inertia of the articulators the first guesture may not be completed before the next one is begun. Consequently the acoustic pattern of each phoneme will vary considerably depending on the identity of the neighbouring phonemes. In some instances an articulator, which is not needed for the production of the current phoneme, will anticipate the following phoneme by moving into a position appropriate for its production. This may well modify the acoustic pattern of the current phoneme to a considerable extent. This simultaneous movement of several articulators to position themselves for the coming sequence of phonemes is known as co-articulation (Öhman, 1966).

Distinctive features

So far only those methods of analysis applicable to physical signals have been considered. The phoneme, a linguistic term, has been used to designate the various categories of speech sounds. It was pointed out earlier that this term is defined by allowing two phonemes to be distinct only if by substituting one for the other in a word, can the meaning of the word be changed. Thus /p/ and /b/ are different phonemes because 'pill' /p ɪ l/ and 'bill' /bɪl/ are different words. Speech sounds which are physically different are not necessarily different phonemes. For example, the noise burst of /k/ in 'key' /ki/ has its energy concentrated at a higher frequency than the /k/ in 'coo' /ku/. If the /k/ of /ku/ is substituted for the /k/ of /ki/ no change in the meaning of the word occurs, so the two versions of /k/ are allophones of the same phoneme. Phonemes can thus be thought of as the elements, or atoms, of language.

The phonemes /p/ and /b/, however, are considered more similar than /p/ and /d/, and yet these are more similar than /p/ and /ɪ/. These similarities and differences can be quantified by describing each phoneme by a bundle of "distinctive features" (Jakobson et al., 1952). The phonemes /p/ and /b/ differ only in that /b/ is voiced and /p/ is voiceless. They differ in the feature "voiced". The phonemes /p/ and /d/ differ not only in the feature "voiced", but also in the place of articulation; /p/ is labial and /d/ is alveolar. In the original formulation of distinctive features (Jakobson et al., 1952) the features were binary oppositions of traditional phonetic terms (Table 4.4). Thus /p/ was "tense" and /b/ was "lax", while /b/ was "grave" and /d/ was "acute". The phoneme /p/ differed from /d/ in the features "tense/lax" and "grave/acute".

Contextual constraints

As phonemes are the "atoms", or building blocks, of speech, an utterance can always be expressed as a string of phonemes. The normal pattern in English is: C_1VC_2

Fig. 4.15(a). Sonagrams of the voiced stops /b,d,g/.

/p/ /t/ /k/

Fig. 5.15(b). Sonagrams of the voicless stops /p,t,k/.

Table 4.4 Distinctive features of the phonemes of English (Jakobson *et al.*, 1952)

	ʊ	æ	ɛ	ʌ	I	l	ŋ	ʃ	tʃ	k	ʒ	dʒ	g	m	f	p	v	b	n	s	θ	t	z	ð	d	h
1. Vocalic /Non-vocalic	+	+	+	+	+	+	−	−	−	−	−	−	−	−	−	−	−	−	−	−	−	−	−	−	−	−
2. Consonantal /Non-consonantal	−	−	−	−	−	+	+	+	+	+	+	+	+	+	+	+	+	+	+	+	+	+	+	+	+	+
3. Compact /Diffuse	+	+	+	−	−		+	+	+	+	+	+	+	−	−	−	−	−	−	−	−	−	−	−	−	−
4. Grave /Acute	+	+	−	+	+	−								+	+	+	+	+	−	−	−	−	−	−	−	−
5. Flat /Plain	+	−		+	−																					
6. Nasal /Oral							+	−	−	−	−	−	−	+	−	−	−	−	+	−	−	−	−	−	−	
7. Tense /Lax								+	+	+	−	−	−		+	+	−	−		+	+	+	−	−	−	+
8. Continuant /Interrupted								+	−	−	+	−	−		+	−	+	−		+	+	−	+	+	−	
9. Strident /Mellow								+	+	−	+	+	−							+	−	−	+	−	−	

$C_1 V C_2 \ldots$, where C_1 is an initial consonant, V is a vowel and C_2 is a final consonant. C_1 and C_2 may also be consonant clusters, and V may also be a diphthong. In English, and in other languages, there are only a certain number of sequences of consonants which occur. In part this is a function of the language, and in part it is because of the unpronouncability of certain combinations. All of the consonantal phonemes, except /ʒ/ and /ŋ/, are found in initial position. The phoneme /ʒ/ occurs in pre-vowel position but only in the middle of words. The stop consonants are only followed by semivowels in pre-vowel position. The allowed combinations are shown in Table 4.5.

The nasals may only be followed by the phoneme /j/ in pre-vowel position. This is also true of the fricatives /f/, /θ/, /ʃ/, /h/, /v/, and the affricate /tʃ/. The semi vowels, the fricatives /z/, /ʒ/, /ð/ and the affricate /dʒ/ only occur singly in pre-vowel position. The phoneme /s/ is the most prolific combiner, being able to precede most non-fricative consonantal clusters. Most of the consonantal phonemes occur in final or post-vowel position. The exceptions are the semivowels /w,r,j/ (/l/ occurs, but it is a different allophone from the pre-vowel one) and the fricatives /h/ and /ʒ/. The fricative /s/ may follow most voiceless phonemes in order to form the plural, and similarly /z/ may follow most voiced phonemes. Some of the combinations are very rare (e.g. /lfθs/ in "twelfths") and some are archaic (/dst/ in "hadst").

It is important to realize that a consonant is part of a cluster when examining sonagrams or otherwise analysing speech. The physical form of /t/ in the word "stop" is much more like /d/ in the isolated syllable /dʊ/ than /t/ in the syllable /tʊ/. Since the combination /sd/ does not occur in English, no confusion normally arises.

Table 4.5. Phoneme sequences in English

Initial consonant clusters

/b/ /bl/ /br/ /bj/ /d/ /dr/ /dj/ /dw/ /g/ /gl/ /gr/ /gj/ /gw/ /p/ /pl/ /pr/ /pj/ /t/ /tr/ /tw/
/tj/ /k/ /kl/ /kr/ /kw/ /kj/ /m/ /mj/ /n/ /nj/ /w/ /r/ /l/ /j/ /f/ /fr/ /fj/ /fl/ /θ/ /θj/ /θr/
/θw/ /s/ /sp/ /st/ /sk/ /sf/ /sm/ /sn/ /sl/ /sw/ /sj/ /spl/ /spr/ /spj/ /str/ /stj/ /skr/ /skj/
/skw/ /ʃ/ /ʃr/ /h/ /hj/ /v/ /vj/ /z/ /ʒ/ /tʃ/ /tʃj/ /dʒ/ /ð/

Final consonant clusters

/b/ /bd/ /bz/ /d/ /dθ/ /dz/ /dst/ /g/ /gd/ /gz/ /p/ /pt/ /pθ/ /ps/ /t/ /ts/ /tθ/ /k/ /kt/ /ks/
/kst/ /ksθ/ /ksθs/ /m/ /mp/ /mf/ /mθ/ /mz/ /md/ /mpts/ /n/ /nt/ /nʃ/ /ns/ /nθ/ /nd/ /nz/
/ndθ/ /ndʒ/ /nst/ /ndθs/ /ndz/ /ŋ/ /ŋk/ /ŋd/ /ŋz/ /ŋkθ/ /ŋkt/ /ŋks/ /l/ /lp/ /lt/ /lk/ /lf/
/lʃ/ /lm/ /ls/ /lθ/ /lb/ /ld/ /lv/ /lz/ /lpt/ /lkt/ /lks/ /lst/ /lfθ/ /lfθs/ /f/ /ft/ /fs/ /fθ/ /θ/ /θt/
/θs/ /s/ /sp/ /st/ /sk/ /ʃ/ /ʃt/ /v/ /vd/ /vz/ /z/ /zd/ /ð/ /ðd/ /ðz/ /tʃ/ /tʃt/ /dʒ/ /dʒd/
/ʒd/.

Statistics of spoken English

There are many difficulties in measuring the relative frequency with which the various phonemes occur in spoken English. Ideally a large number of conversations should be recorded, then these should be transcribed by phoneticians and counts should be made of each phoneme. In everyday speech many sentences are left unfinished. In American telephone conversations French *et al.* (1930) have estimated that 20 per cent of the words are "uh", and "ah", and "yeah". If these are included the

Table 4.6. The frequency of occurrence of the phonemes
of English (Denes, 1963)

Vowels and diphthongs		Consonants	
/ə/	9.0445	/t/	8.4033
/ɪ/	8.2537	/n/	7.0849
/ɑi/	2.8473	/s/	5.0893
/ɛ/	2.8126	/d/	4.1767
/i/	1.7878	/l/	3.6892
/əʊ/	1.7477	/m/	3.2890
/ʌ/	1.6701	/ð/	2.9927
/ɒ/	1.5330	/k/	2.8985
/æ/	1.5261	/r/	2.7697
/ɛi/	1.4956	/w/	2.5661
/u/	1.4222	/z/	2.4927
/ɔ/	1.2007	/b/	2.0842
/ɑ/	0.7755	/v/	1.8515
/ɑʊ/	0.7741	/p/	1.7698
/ʊ/	0.7672	/f/	1.7283
/ɜ/	0.6661	/h/	1.6729
/ɛə/	0.4335	/j/	1.5303
/iə/	0.2867	/ŋ/	1.2436
/uə/	0.1426	/g/	1.1619
/ɔi/	0.0872	/ʃ/	0.7021
		/θ/	0.5955
Total	39.2742	/dʒ/	0.5138
		/tʃ/	0.3684
		/ʒ/	0.0512
		Total	60.7256

phonemes of which they are composed will dominate the counts, and the frequencies obtained will not be very helpful when a typical sentence is considered.

One useful estimation of the statistics of spoken English has been made by Denes (1963). He used as his source two books written in phonetic spelling for the use of foreign speakers learning to pronounce English. These contained a total of 72,210 phonemes. The frequency of occurrence of the forty-four phonemes of Received Pronunciation is given in Table 4.6. As might be expected the most commonly occurring phoneme is the central vowel /ə/, and the second most common is the consonant /t/.

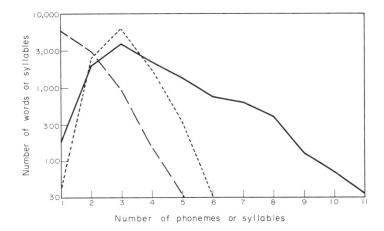

Fig. 4.17. Number of words as a function of number of phonemes per word (solid curve) and syllables per word (dashed curve), and number of syllables as a function of number of phonemes per syllable (dotted curve) for words or syllables with stress.

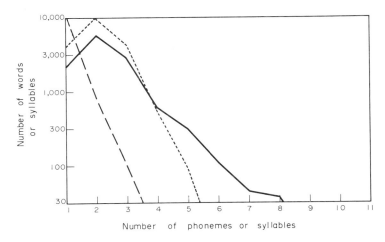

Fig. 4.18. Number of words as a function of number of phonemes per word (solid curve) and syllables per word (dashed curve) and number of syllables as a function of phonemes per syllable (dotted curve) for words or syllables without stress.

The nine most commonly occurring phonemes /ə,t,ɪ,n,s,d,l,m,ð/ make up over 50 per cent of the phonemes of a typical utterance.

Denes has also calculated the relative frequency of occurrence of stressed vowels, unstressed vowels and consonants. Figure 4.17 shows the numbers of words occurring in his data as a function of the number of phonemes and syllables in the word, and of syllables as a function of the number of phonemes for stressed words or syllables, and Fig. 4.18 shows the equivalent data for words or syllables without stress.

It is of interest in speech recognition to know the relative frequency with which one phoneme follows another. This is a measure of the predictability of the second phoneme from the occurrence of the first. To this end, Denes has calculated the digram frequencies of phoneme pairs.

Another statistic which is of interest in speech recognition is the distribution of minimal pairs. This is the frequency of occurrence of pairs of phonemes which, if one is substituted for the other, forms a second allowable word. For example, if /b/ is substituted for /p/ in /pig/, a valid word /big/ results. Thus /p/ and /b/ form a minimal pair. This statistic has also been computed by Denes for his 72,210 phonemes. The effect of the age of the speaker on the statistics of phonemes of American English has been investigated by Carterette and Jones (1974).

CHAPTER 5

Speech Synthesis

Historical

One of the most useful tools for studying speech recognition is a speech synthesizer. It was only when such machines had been developed to a stage where they could be used to generate speech-like sounds for psychoacoustical experiments, that the acoustic cues which are employed in speech recognition were isolated.

Interest in the construction of machines which reproduce the human voice goes back for at least two centuries. In 1779 Kratzenstein constructed a set of acoustic resonators which, when driven by a vibrating reed, produced imitations of the vowels (Paget, 1930). A more elaborate machine was built by von Kempelen in 1791. This consisted of a pair of bellows which supplied a stream of air to a reed, which in turn excited a leather tube. This tube was held in the hand, and manipulated to imitate the resonances of the vocal tract. Extra tubes and whistles were added to imitate the nasal and fricative sounds. An improved version was later built and exhibited by Wheatstone (Dudley and Tarnoczy, 1950; Flanagan, 1972). This model was seen by A. M. Bell, who was so impressed that he constructed a talking machine of his own (Bell, 1922).

Vocoders

More successful talking machines were not produced until the development of electronics. One of the first electrical synthesizers was the Voder (Fig. 5.1). With this, a trained operator could "play" the keys like an organ, and produce intelligible speech (Flanagan, 1972). The "resonance" box, simulating the vocal tract, contained ten band-pass filters. The keys controlled potentiometers. By pressing each of the keys by the right amount, the spectrum of the source (a pulse train or random noise) could be modified to reproduce each of the continuous sounds of speech. Special keys were used to generate the stop consonants, and a foot pedal was employed to control the "pitch" of the voice.

In telephone engineering it was realized that the information needed to generate a speech sound is less than the information needed to transmit the waveform. Thus a sound could be analysed into components, parameters of the components transmitted, then the sound synthesized at the receiving end. If the parameters can be transmitted over a channel of a smaller bandwidth than the channel required to transmit the original signal, a "bandwidth compression" system results.

One such system is the vocoder (Dudley, 1939). This is shown schematically in Fig. 5.2. The analyser consists of a set of band-pass filters covering the frequency range of

59

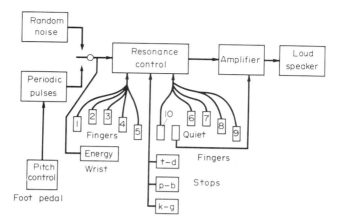

Fig. 5.1. Schematic diagram of the Voder synthesizer.

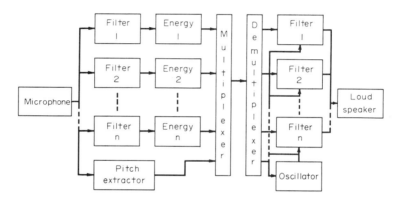

Fig. 5.2. Block diagram of the Vocoder (Dudley, 1939).

speech. The amplitude of the signal in each of the bands is measured continuously, and so is the excitation frequency of the speech (FO) and a decision as to whether the sound is "voiced" or not (SW). These parameters (the amplitudes of the signals in the bands, FO and SW) are multiplexed and transmitted to the receiver. Here the parameters are demultiplexed, and the amplitude parameters are used to control the gains of a similar set of band-pass filters excited by a pulse train (controlled by FO) or a noise source, selected by SW. With ten to twenty channels in each of the filter bands, intelligible speech can result. The main difficulty is in tracking the fundamental frequency. This is easier for some voices than others, and generally more difficult for female voices than male ones. In order to circumvent this difficulty other devices such as the voice-excited vocoder (Schroeder and David, 1960) have been invented. In this device, the low-frequency part of the spectrum is transmitted intact, and used to excite the filters of the synthesizer. This improves the quality of the synthesized speech, but at the expense of more bandwidth for transmission.

Pattern playback

The vocoder principle, the synthesis of speech-like sounds from a pattern of slowly varying signals, has been of great utility in the study of speech perception. It has enabled speech-like stimuli to be generated, and the effects of manipulating features of these stimuli to be listened to. Thus the features of speech sounds which are important for perception have been deduced. One of the earliest devices used in the study of speech perception was "Pattern playback", built at the Haskins Laboratories (Cooper *et al.*, 1951). The operating principle is shown in Fig. 5.3. A variable density tonewheel

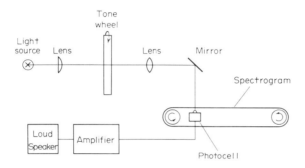

Fig. 5.3. Operating principle of Pattern Playback.

modulates a thin sheet of light, and produces a 120-Hz fundamental together with its first fifty harmonics. These are reflected onto a plastic sheet. On this sheet is painted the spectrogram of the sound to be synthesized. The light normally passes through the sheet but when the spectrogram passes under it the light is reflected by the pattern and is collected by a photocell. The output of this is amplified and converted to sound by a loudspeaker. The sounds produced by this device all have a constant "pitch" of 120 Hz, but in other respects they resemble speech sounds and are fairly intelligible.

Formant synthesizers

Instead of specifying the spectrum of a speech signal by the energies in a set of band-pass filters, the shape can be described by a set of parameters giving the frequencies and amplitudes of the formants. (This is sufficient for vowel sounds, but for some consonants the zeros, as well as the poles, should be specified for a complete description.) If these parameters are measured continuously, together with others representing the frequency and nature of the excitation source, and then these parameters are used to synthesize speech, a new kind of bandwidth compression system results. This is known as the "formant vocoder". On theoretical grounds it requires less bandwidth than the channel vocoder because parameters describing only the first three or four formants need be transmitted. In practice, however, it has been less used than the channel vocoder because of the complexity and cost of the circuitry required to track the formant parameters. The synthesizer part of the formant vocoder has proved extremely useful in experiments on speech perception. The excitation frequency of formant synthesizers can be controlled in the same way as the other parameters, and this increased flexibility has caused formant synthesizers to replace other devices, such as Pattern playback, almost entirely for this purpose.

One of the first formant synthesizers, PAT (Parametric Artificial Talker), was demonstrated by Lawrence (1953) in 1952. About the same time Fant developed the OVE II synthesizer in Sweden (Fant and Mártony, 1962). A schematic diagram of a later version of PAT (Anthony and Lawrence, 1962) is shown in Fig. 5.4. It consists of

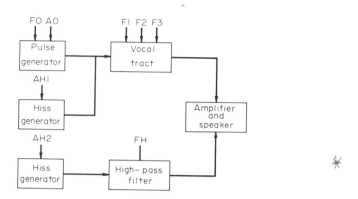

Fig. 5.4. Block diagram of the Parametric Artificial Talker (F1, F2, F3 are the formant frequencies, F0 and A0 the frequency and amplitude of the excitation signal, AH1 the amplitude of the hiss through formants signal, and FH the cut-off frequency of the high-pass filter).

three resonant circuits in series, whose centre frequencies are dynamically controlled, excited by a pulse generator or a hiss generator. The repetition frequency and amplitude of the pulses, and the amplitude of the hiss, are dynamically controlled by external voltages. By adjusting the frequencies of the resonant circuits to appropriate values, a series of steady-state vowels can be produced. The pitch and loudness can be controlled by the pulse generator parameters. The hiss generator can be used to produce aspirated sounds or whispered vowels. The other branch of the synthesizer is used to generate fricative sounds. A second hiss generator excites a high-pass filter whose cut-off frequency can be controlled.

An alternative to the series-coupled formant synthesizer shown in Fig. 5.4 is the parallel coupled type (Fig. 5.5). Each has advantages for certain applications (Holmes, 1972). The series type is a better analogy of the vocal tract, and produces vowels in which the relative amplitudes of the formants are automatically determined (Fant, 1956). It can produce natural-sounding speech and, because only the amplitudes of the source rather than the amplitudes of each formant need be specified, it requires less control parameters than the parallel type, and so may be preferred in a formant vocoder system. On the other hand, individual control of formant amplitudes makes the parallel type preferable for the synthesis of certain consonants. As a tool for speech perception experiments, this extra flexibility can be very useful. Holmes (1973) has demonstrated that parallel-coupled synthesizers are capable of generating synthetic speech of high quality.

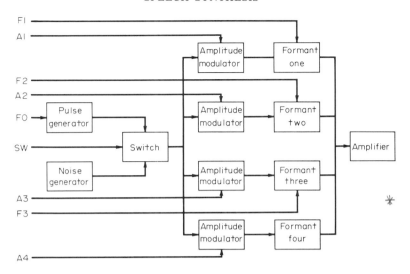

Fig. 5.5. Block diagram of a parallel-coupled formant synthesizer.

Control of speech synthesizers

At the time when PAT and OVE II were first built there were no function generators readily available which could supply the control voltages. An ingeneous device was built by Fourcin (1960) to control PAT. The parameters were drawn as time varying functions in conducting ink on a plastic sheet. This sheet ran between the rollers of a mangle, one of whose rollers was coated with a conducting material which had a uniform potential gradient across it. As the sheet ran between the rollers the potential of the ink track varied with the point of contact of the roller. This potential was sensed, amplified and used to control the appropriate parameter of PAT.

When digital computers became generally available these were used to store and modify parameter data. At first they were used indirectly. Holmes *et al.* (1964) generated parameter data on punched paper tape, then employed a high-speed photoelectric reader to generate the voltages for their synthesizer. Later synthesizers were coupled directly to computers via digital-to-analogue converters. Some synthesizers are now digitally controlled (Liljencrants, 1968). Various methods have been employed to get the parameter data into the computer. With curve-followers this can be done directly from sonagrams. An alternative method is to employ a light pen (Tomlinson, 1966; Ainsworth, 1967a). This has the advantage that the parameter data can be viewed with a computer display, modified with a light pen, and the resulting synthesized speech can be heard immediately.

Digital synthesis

Instead of building an analogue speech synthesizer and controlling it by means of a digital computer, it is possible to perform the synthesis entirely by digital hardware. Either a general purpose computer can be programmed to perform the synthesis

(Flanagan, 1972) or a special purpose digital computer can be constructed (Rabiner *et al.*, 1971). In either case the principle is the same and is similar to that used in the design of analogue synthesizers. It is shown in Fig. 5.6.

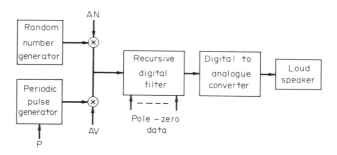

Fig. 5.6. Principle of the digital synthesizer (P is the pulse repetition rate, AV the amplitude for voiced sounds, and AN the amplitude for voiceless sounds).

A random number generator simulates the source for voiceless sounds, and a counter is used to produce the pulses for voiced sounds. These sources are modified by a recursive filter whose coefficients are determined by the speech formants as they change with time. Three variable resonances are typically used for voiced sounds, and a pole-zero combination for voiceless sounds. The digital numbers produced are converted to analogue voltages which drive a loudspeaker to produce audible sounds.

The recursive filter generates quantized samples of the speech signal, represented by binary numbers. The filter can be implemented by digital operations in a number of ways, one of which is to represent the resonances and anti-resonances by second-order difference equations (Flanagan, 1972). Digital synthesizers have the advantage of being less prevalent to drift than their analogue counterparts. The programmed type is also more flexible, as additional resonances can readily be added by changing the program. Their disadvantage is that they may not produce speech in real-time.

Linear predictive coding

A digital technique which has been developed as a bandwidth compression system for transmitting speech is linear predictive coding (LPC). In the analyser the speech wave is sampled and quantized as shown in Fig. 5.7. The poles (or poles and zeros) of the spectrum are calculated. These coefficients are also estimated by linear prediction from their previous values. The differences between the calculated and predicted values of the coefficients are transmitted to the synthesizer. The synthesizer contains a linear predictor which is identical with the one in the analyser. This predicts the coefficients, which are then modified by the error signals transmitted to the synthesizer, and used to synthesize the speech signal. Twice as many coefficients as there are formants in the spectrum are required (Atal and Schroeder, 1970).

LPC has proved to be a highly efficient bandwidth compression system. It does, however, suffer from one of the same difficulties as vocoders. It requires a good fundamental frequency tracking device. Given this, and a sufficient number of predictor

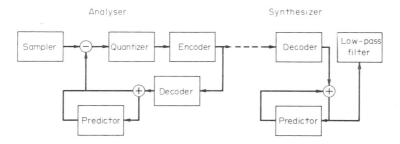

Fig. 5.7. Block diagram of a predictive coding system.

coefficients (at least 13), good-quality speech is generated by the synthesizer. Better-quality speech can be produced if a pole-zero model, rather than an all-pole model, is employed. A large number of zeros are required, however, before the quality is noticeably better than with an all-pole model. There are additional difficulties with the analysis, if the zeros are to be determined (Atal and Schroeder, 1974).

Vocal tract synthesizers

Formant synthesizers attempt to generate signals which have the same acoustic characteristics as the speech sounds which emanate from the lips. They make no attempt, except for the separation of the excitation source from the vocal tract transfer function, to simulate the human speech production apparatus. For this reason formant synthesizers are sometimes known as "terminal analogue" speech synthesizers. An alternative approach is to build an analogue of the vocal tract. The method employed is to divide the tract into a number of sections, each short enough to be considered of uniform cross-section. About twenty to thirty sections is sufficient. Each section can be represented by an impedance network which has the same transfer function as that section (Fig. 5.8). The values in the elements of the network can be derived from the dimensions and physical properties of the vocal tract (Flanagan, 1965).

Passive devices of this kind, capable of producing steady-state sounds, have been constructed by Dunn (1950) and Fant (1960). The vocal tract shapes necessary for producing vowel sounds have been determined by Fant by high-speed X-ray photography. Dynamic devices, capable of producing continuous speech, have been designed

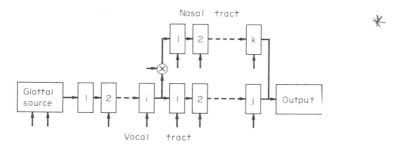

Fig. 5.8. Block diagram of a vocal tract synthesizer.

by Rosen (1958) and Hecker (1962). Control of such a device can be by means of a digital computer (Dennis, 1962).

Speech synthesis by rule

In recent years attention in speech synthesis research has shifted from the design of electronic synthesizers to the synthesis of the parameters which control them. Analysis of speech sounds and experiments on the perception of vowels and consonants has enabled an inventory of the parameters necessary for synthesizing each of the phonemes of English to be drawn up (Liberman *et al.*, 1959). This information has been programmed into a computer, and rules have been devised which enable the appropriate values of parameters for the synthesis of a given string of phonemes to be calculated automatically. The first computer programmes of this type were written by Kelly and Gerstman (1961) and Holmes *et al.* (1964).

A recent program for synthesis-by-rule has been written by Ainsworth (1972b). It uses a small digital computer controlling a formant synthesizer of the type shown in Fig. 5.5. The program contains a look-up table which has ten numbers for each of the phonetic elements. Eight of these represent the steady-state values of each of the following parameters of that element: SW, F1, A1, F2, A2, F3, A3, A4. The two other numbers are duration parameters. T1 represents the duration of the steady-state part of the element and T2 the duration of the transition from one element to the next. The duration parameters are quantized in 10-msec intervals. A sequence of characters, representing the string of phonemes of the utterance to be synthesized, is typed into the computer. The first phonetic element is read, and sufficient steady-state values of the parameters are deposited in a file so that when sent to the synthesizer they will generate an appropriate sound for a time T1. The next phonetic element is then read, and values are calculated for each parameter every 10 msec so that it will change in a linear fashion in a time T2 from its steady-state value in the first element ($P_i(1)$) to its steady-state value in the second element ($P_i(2)$):

$$P_i(n) = \frac{[P_i(2) - P_i(1)]n}{T2(1)}$$

where n is the number of 10-msec intervals since the end of the steady-state portion of the first element. These values are deposited in the file, followed by the steady-state values of the second element for the new T1. The third element is read, the transitional values are calculated, and the program continues in this manner until the last element in the sequence has been processed.

The result is a file of numbers which, when sent via a multiplexer and digital-to-analogue converters, produces nine time-varying voltages which control the synthesizer. The speech produced by this system is normally intelligible, especially with a little practice at listening (Ainsworth, 1974c).

More sophisticated systems which allow each element in the sequence to be modified by its neighbours, and which contain more natural rules for synthesizing stress and intonation patterns, have been described by Mattingly (1971) and Coker (1968) for American English. A particularly successful system has been produced by Carlson and

Granström (1974) for Swedish. Other systems have been made for Dutch by Willems (1974), Debiasi *et al.* (1974) for Italian, and for other languages.

Transmission of speech signals

The channel capacity required for the transmission of a signal is given by

$$C = W \log_2 (1 + S/N)$$

where W is the bandwidth of the channel, S is the amplitude of the signal, N is the amplitude of the noise and C is measured in bits per sec (Shannon and Weaver, 1963). Speech contains components in the frequency range from 50 Hz to 10,000 Hz. The loudest speech sounds are about 50 dB greater than the quietest. Hence the channel capacity required to transmit a speech waveform undistorted is about 100,000 bits per sec.

In a telephone system the bandwidth is usually limited to about 3 kHz and the signal-to-noise ratio is reduced, perhaps to 30 dB. Intelligible speech can, therefore, be transmitted by a channel of about 15,000 bits per sec. A high-quality channel vocoder might have twenty channels, each having a bandwidth of about 50 Hz and quantization to 100 levels (seven bits). This would require a channel capacity of 6000 bits per sec, although successful vocoders have been built with channel capacities of 2000 bits per sec (Meeker and Nelson, 1964).

Jordan and Kelly (1974) have demonstrated that linear predictive coding can produce about the same quality of speech as a channel vocoder provided that there are the same number of coefficients in the LPC system as there are channels in the vocoder. A formant vocoder can operate with about eight parameters quantized to five bits, with each parameter channel bandlimited to 50 Hz. A channel capacity of about 2000 bits per sec is required. Some of the parameters may be adequately specified by less than five bits, so this figure might be reduced somewhat. Further reductions in channel capacity can be achieved by a variable-frame-rate coding scheme (McLarnon and Holmes, 1974).

CHAPTER 6

Vowel Recognition

Speech synthesizers, similar to the types described in Chapter 5, have been used in a great number of experiments to discover the features of each phoneme which are important for recognizing it or for distinguishing it from other phonemes. It is possible to discover the characteristic features of a phoneme by analysis, but it is only by synthesizing the sound and listening to it that the features necessary for perception can be ascertained.

By this method Delattre *et al.* (1952) showed that the frequencies of the lowest two formants are the most important features for recognizing a vowel. They synthesized vowels containing one, two and more formants, and found that two formants were necessary in order to produce a complete set of vowels. With one formant they could produce only back vowels. With more than two formants more natural sounding vowels could be produced, but the full set of American English vowels could be synthesized with just two formants.

Dimensional analysis

It might be argued that formants are products of the method of production of vowel sounds (they are, after all, the resonances of the vocal tract) and that they have nothing to do with perception. Or, if they have, that the true perceptual features are some combination of formant frequencies. An ingeneous method was devised by Pols *et al.* (1969) to determine the dimensions of vowel perception without imposing any preconceived ideas about formants being involved. They recorded a set of Dutch vowels, and then measured the similarities between them using the method of triadic comparisons. In this method three vowel sounds were played to a listener who was asked to judge which pair of vowels were most similar. All combinations of vowels were tested, and a similarity matrix was constructed. A dimensional analysis was performed on this matrix in order to determine how many orthogonal dimensions are necessary in order to explain the differences between the vowels. They found that two dimensions explained 70 per cent of the variance, three dimensions 80 per cent, and four dimensions 90 per cent. Pols *et al.* then analysed the same vowel sounds using a set of third octave filters. These were chosen because their bandwidths approximate to the critical bands found to be important in auditory perception (Chapter 3). A dimensional analysis was performed on the outputs of these filters, and the principal components determined. When the vowels were plotted in a two-dimensional space determined by the two most important components, similar plots resulted for both the physical and perceptual data. Furthermore, yet another similar plot resulted when the first two formant frequencies were plotted along the two dimensions. The first principal component was identified with the frequency of the second formant and the second principal component with the frequency of the first formant.

Formant frequency estimation

We can conceive of the identification of a vowel being determined by its position in a multidimensional space. The principal dimensions of this space are the frequency of the first formant (F1) and the frequency of the second formant (F2). If a set of vowel sounds are synthesized having every combination of F1 in the range 220 to 1000 Hz and F2 in the range 750 to 2600 Hz, and presented to a group of listeners for identification, the boundaries between the vowels in a two-dimensional perceptual space can be determined. Figure 6.1 shows a typical result of such an experiment with F1 quantized

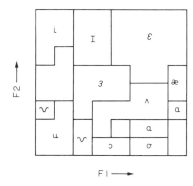

Fig. 6.1. Typical result of an experiment in which listeners were asked to identify synthetic vowels.

to 120 Hz and F2 to 240 Hz making a total of sixty-four stimulus sounds in the set.

It will be noted that the centre of each area corresponds approximately with the position of each vowel in an F1–F2 space as determined by measurements of formant frequencies of naturally produced vowel sounds.

This experimental technique can be used to explore the way in which other parameters of synthesized vowels affect vowel perception. The experiment is repeated a number of times with different values of the parameter concerned, and its effect on the perceptual vowel areas is determined directly (Ainsworth and Millar, 1971).

One such parameter of interest is formant amplitude. Delattre *et al.* (1952) found that when the second formant of a synthesized front vowel was reduced to zero amplitude, the corresponding back vowel was perceived. The above technique was employed by Ainsworth and Millar (1972) to explore the perceptual effects as the second formant amplitude was systematically reduced. It was hypothesized that the frequencies of the formants might be estimated by the perceptual mechanism either by picking the peaks in the spectrum or by some process analogous to taking moments. In the former case it would be expected that the identity of each stimulus would remain constant until the second formant amplitude was reduced to the level of the noise, then change abruptly to the corresponding back vowel, whereas in the latter case the estimated value of F2 would change more gradually, so the centre of the vowel area would gradually shift to a lower position. The results indicated an abrupt change, supporting the peak-picking hypothesis. It was found that the amplitude of the second formant could be reduced to about 28 dB below that of the first formant before the change in vowel identity took place.

There is a third alternative hypothesis which would also be supported by the abrupt change in results. This is that there is a moment-taking mechanism for determining the frequency of each formant, but it is confined to the range of each formant. If the restriction were performed with the aid of a set of "weights", the mathematics of the process would be similar to the multidimensional scaling techniques employed by Pols *et al.* (1969) in their analysis of Dutch vowels.

The possibility of the formant frequency being estimated by a weighted sum of harmonics rather than by picking the most prominent harmonic has been investigated by Carlson *et al.* (1974). They varied the fundamental frequency so that the harmonics shifted but the spectrum envelope remained constant (Fig. 6.2), and measured the

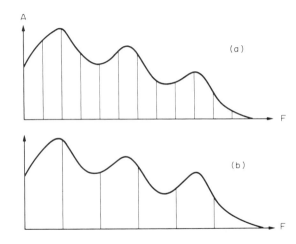

Fig. 6.2. Spectrum of two vowels having the same envelope, but the fundamental frequency of (a) is half that of (b).

position of the perceptual boundary between two Swedish vowel sounds. They concluded from their results that a listener could use some interpolation mechanism to estimate the formant frequency as opposed to a selection of the loudest or most significant harmonic.

Formant transitions

Although the foregoing experiments suggest that the formant frequencies are the main factors in the recognition of isolated vowels, the situation is somewhat more complex in connected speech. The speed at which the articulators can move is limited by their inertia. Consequently there is sometimes insufficient time for a steady vowel configuration to be reached before the shape of the tract must be changed to articulate the next consonant. In such circumstances the frequencies of the formants do not reach their target values. This phenomenon is known as "vowel reduction" (Lindblom, 1963). Listeners, however, do not appear to confuse the identity of the intended vowel sound. Lindblom and Studdert-Kennedy (1967) synthesized syllables containing the vowels /ɪ/ and /ʊ/ between the consonants /w/ (which has a low initial value of F2) and /j/ (high value of F2), i.e. /wVw/ and /jVj/. Listeners placed the boundaries between /ɪ/ and /ʊ/ at different frequencies in the two conditions. It is suggested that the listeners used not only the frequencies of the formants, but also their direction and rate of change, in order to allow for the implied sluggishness in the production mechanism. Cortical neurones which respond only to changes in frequency, similar to those found in the auditory system of animals, could form the physical basis of such a mechanism.

Vowel duration

The duration of the vowel sound is influenced by its consonantal environment as well as by the tempo and stress pattern of the sentence in which it occurs. It is therefore difficult by analysis alone to ascertain the importance of duration as a cue for recognition. Peterson and Lehiste (1960), however, have shown that when these factors are subtracted or neutralized the resulting syllabic nuclei fall into two classes which may be termed "long" and "short".

Experiments involving the perception of vowels in which durational cues have been removed by making the sounds very long or very short have produced ambiguous results concerning the importance of duration. Seigenthaler (1950) obtained recognition scores of about 50 per cent with sustained vowels, yet Hyde (1969) has reported that vowel segments almost as brief as a single glottal period can be correctly identified. Cohen et al. (1967) found that the three factors, first and second formant frequency and duration, have to be combined in an optional way for maximal recognition of synthetic vowels. Other investigators have suggested that duration may be a more important factor for the recognition of some vowels than others. Bennett (1968) has shown that duration can be an important cue in distinguishing between certain vowels which have a similar spectral form, and Stevens (1959) reported that duration does not much affect discrimination of pairs of close vowels but that it may affect other pairs of vowels. With a set of vowels covering the F1–F2 space Ainsworth (1972a) found that the centres of the vowel areas remained constant as the duration of the vowels in the set was changed. The areas themselves, however, were affected. As the duration of the vowels in the set was increased, the proportion of "long" vowels increased and the proportion of "short" vowels decreased.

The duration of vowels varies considerably in fast and slow speech. It is thus possible that when duration is used as a cue for the recognition of a vowel, it is the duration of the vowel relative to the other syllables in the utterance, rather than its absolute duration, which is important. In order to test this hypothesis Ainsworth (1974b) repeated the previous experiment but preceded the test vowel by a sequence of sounds whose tempo could be varied. He found that there was a contrast effect. When the preceding sounds were of brief duration, a greater proportion of "long" vowels were heard, and vice versa. Moreover, those vowels whose identity depended strongly on duration were more sensitive to this effect. The effect was small, but significant, and was independent of the identity of the vowel sound in the precursive sequence.

Vocal tract normalization

Peterson and Barney (1952) measured the formant frequencies and amplitudes of the vowels in monosyllabic words spoken by a number of men, women, and children. When the frequencies of the first two formants of all the speakers were plotted against each other, there was a considerable overlap in the areas occupied by the vowels. If the frequencies of the first two formants are the only features of the vowels which are used to recognize them, the vowels in the areas of overlap would be ambiguous. However, listeners normally have no difficulty in understanding the speech of many talkers, so it is likely that the perceptual mechanism somehow normalizes speech sounds so that the variation between individual talkers is reduced.

The fundamental frequency of vowels produced by children is about an octave higher than those produced by men, whereas the frequencies of the formants are about 30 per cent higher. This latter is due to the shorter vocal tracts of children, and accounts for much of the spread in Peterson and Barney's results. The correlation between fundamental frequency and formant frequency suggests that fundamental frequency could be used to derive the normalization factor, and there is some evidence to support this view. Miller (1953) showed that when the fundamental of synthetic vowels was doubled there was a shift in the categorization of some vowels near perceptual boundaries even though the spectrum envelopes of the test sounds remained unchanged.

Fujisaki and Kawashima (1968) explored the magnitude of this shift for Japanese vowels. They found that if the fundamental frequency was varied alone, the shift in the perceptual boundaries between pairs of vowels was too small for complete normalization, but if the frequency of the third formant was varied in conjunction with the fundamental frequency the shift was of the correct magnitude.

Similar experiments with English speakers have given less clear results. Slawson (1968), in a scaling experiment, found that when the fundamental frequency was increased by an octave the preferred increases in first and second formant frequency were only about 10 per cent. In an experiment similar to that of Fujisaki and Kawashima but with English listeners, Ainsworth (1974a) found great individual variation in the shift of perceptual boundaries between pairs of vowels. For some listeners the shift was negligible, whilst for others it was greater than that required by the normalization hypothesis.

Another factor which might be employed to aid vocal tract normalization is the frequency of the formants in the part of the utterance which precedes the vowel being perceived. Ladefoged and Broadbent (1960) synthesized the phrase "Please say what this word is" followed by the test word "bet". They then lowered the frequency of the second formant in the carrier phrase (so that it still sounded like the same words, but with a different voice speaking), but kept the formant frequencies in the test word constant. When they played the new carrier phrase the test word was heard as "bit".

Gerstman (1968) has shown that factors derived from the formant frequencies of some vowels are sufficient to normalize the formant frequencies of the others. He analysed the data of Peterson and Barney (1952), and found that if the formants of the vowels of each speaker are normalized in terms of his highest and lowest formant frequencies, an algorithm can be constructed which, using these normalized values, classifies over 97 per cent of the vowels of all speakers correctly. The vowels /i,u,ɑ/ are sufficient to obtain the normalizing factors for each talker.

In order to discover which of these normalizing factors is most important, Ainsworth (1975b) synthesized a set of vowels with every combination of first and second formant frequency. These were presented to listeners preceded by the three vowels /i,u,ɑ/. The fundamental frequency and the formant frequency of the precursor vowels were systematically varied. Assuming that an octave rise in fundamental frequency is equivalent to a 30 per cent rise in formant frequencies, it was found that changing the frequencies of the formants of the precursor vowels produced a shift in the perceptual vowel areas which was about twice as great as that produced by the change in fundamental frequency.

Reliability of vowel perception

The vowel quadrilateral was mentioned in Chapter 1 as a device used by phoneticians for comparing the vowels of different languages. Laver (1965) has used this to determine the reliability of vowel perception. He synthesized a number of vowels, and asked a group of phoneticians to place these on vowel quadrilaterals. He then repeated this on different days with the vowels presented in different orders.

He found that there was very good agreement in the average location of each stimulus by each subject within the group. The scatter of the individual locations suggest an uncertainty, when translated into formant frequencies of about 60 Hz in the first and 120 Hz in the second formant frequencies.

Ainsworth and Millar (1972) have measured this uncertainty by a different technique. They synthesized a set of vowels covering the entire F1–F2 space as described in the earlier part of this chapter. They used naïve listeners, and asked them to indicate in which of a set of given words the perceived vowel sound occurred. This experiment was repeated several times with the stimulus sounds presented in a different order on each occasion. The centres of the measured vowel areas were calculated, and the standard deviation of these centres determined. The standard deviation was found to be 110 Hz for F1 and 183 Hz for F2, considerably greater than Laver's figures.

The experiment was repeated with the stimulus sounds embedded in an "h–d" context. The increased speech-likeness of the stimuli made the listeners' responses more consistent, and the corresponding figures obtained were 44 Hz and 107 Hz. Finally the experiment was repeated with the isolated vowel stimuli. The measured value of the standard deviation of F1 was 60 Hz and of F2 was 121 Hz, which is in complete agreement with Laver.

It might be concluded that these figures represent some limit on the reliability of the perception of isolated synthesized vowels which is the same for all listeners after some training.

Difference limens for vowels

A vowel sound may be described by its fundamental frequency and the amplitude and frequency of each of its formants. One method of estimating the discriminability of vowels is to measure the difference limens for each of these parameters.

Flanagan and Saslow (1958) measured the DL for the fundamental frequency of vowels generated by a speech synthesizer. They found this to be 0.3 to 0.5 per cent of the fundamental frequency for vowels appropriate to a man, i.e. about 0.5 Hz. This is the same order as the DL for pure tones measured by Nordmark (1968).

Flanagan (1955) used a similar technique to measure the DL for formant frequencies. He found that these depend to an important extent on the proximity of the other formants in the vowel. They are of the order of 3 to 5 per cent of the formant frequency for both F1 and F2. This is only slightly less than the accuracy of vowel identification as measured by Laver (1965) and Ainsworth and Millar (1972), suggesting that discrimination and identification of vowel sounds is mediated by the same mechanism.

Flanagan (1957) has also measured the DL for the amplitude of the second formant of a synthesized /æ/ vowel. He concluded that a change of 3 dB in amplitude could just be detected, which is the same order of magnitude as the DL of pure tones (Chapter 3). In relative terms, the DL is about 40 per cent of the second formant amplitude.

It is interesting to note that fundamental frequency, measured as a percentage, is an order of magnitude more discriminable than formant frequency, which in turn is an order of magnitude more discriminable than formant amplitude. The DLs for fundamental frequency and formant amplitude are similar to the corresponding values for a pure tone. The DL for formant frequency, as will be seen in the next chapter, is not constant but depends upon the closeness of the vowel to a perceptual boundary.

CHAPTER 7

Consonant Recognition

The factors involved in the recognition of consonants have been determined by similar methods to those employed for vowels. Firstly, an analysis of spoken versions of the consonants was made in order to find the acoustic features which might be important for distinguishing the consonants from each other. Next, syllables containing the consonants were synthesized. Finally, the acoustic features which are necessary for recognition of the consonants were determined by manipulating the acoustic form of the synthesized stimuli.

Perception of semivowels

The factor which enables the glides /w,r,l,j/ to be distinguished from the other sounds of speech appears to be the duration of the formant transitions. Liberman *et al.* (1956) generated two series of sounds with the pattern-playback synthesizer. One series contained stimuli in which the frequencies of the first and second formants were initially low, but increased to those of the vowel /ɛ/ in a specified time (Fig. 7.1). When

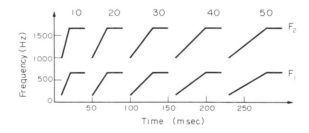

Fig. 7.1. Schematic spectrograms of the stimuli used to produce the /bɛ,wɛ,uɛ/ series.

the formant transitions were sufficiently long, the stimulus was perceived as beginning with a /u/ vowel. As the transitions were shortened to about 150 msec a /w/ was perceived, and for very rapid transitions (less than 50 msec) a /b/ was heard. The other series of stimuli began with a low first formant frequency and a high second. This series was perceived as /iɛ/, then /jɛ/, and finally /gɛ/ as the formant transitions were progressively shortened. The initial phoneme changed from /i/ to /j/ at about 200 msec, and from /j/ to /g/ at 80 msec.

In order to determine whether it is the duration of the formant transitions or their rate of change, another experiment was performed. A number of syllables were synthesized with rising formant transitions, but with different target vowels, so that different rates of change of formant frequency were required to reach the appropriate level in a given time. The results indicated that it is the duration of the formant transitions and not their rate of change which is the important feature.

The features which serve to distinguish between the semivowels have been investigated by O'Connor et al. (1957) for initial position, and by Lisker (1957b) for intervocalic position. They reached the conclusion that it is the initial frequency of the second formant transition which is the main cue which enables this group of phonemes to be distinguished from each other. If the second formant begins at the top of its frequency range (2700 Hz) a /j/ is perceived, and if it begins at bottom (500 Hz) a /w/ is heard. The actual starting frequency, however, depends somewhat on the following vowel. For a /j/ before /i/ the start of F2 must be about 2700 Hz, but before /ɛ/ the start can be lowered to about 2300 Hz. Similarly for a /w/ before /u/ F2 must begin below 500 Hz, but for the remaining vowels it can be raised to about 840 Hz.

For /r/ the frequency range of the F2 onset before /i/ and /ɛ/ was found to be 840–1560 Hz, before /ɔ/ 840–1200 Hz, and before /u/ 600–1200 Hz. For /l/ before /i/ and /ɛ/ the range was 960–1800 Hz, before /æ/ 840–1800 Hz, and before /ɔ/ and /u/ 840–1680 Hz. There is an overlap in the ranges suitable for synthesizing /r/ and /l/. The ambiguity may be resolved by providing /r/ with a rising third formant, and /l/ with a falling or steady one.

O'Connor et al. (1957) were not able to produce a convincing /l/ before the vowel /e/ in their set of stimuli. Ainsworth (1968a) later demonstrated that a more satisfactory /l/ before front vowels could be synthesized if a step-function transition was employed for the first formant instead of the gradual transitions employed in the original stimuli.

Perception of stop consonants

The factors involved in the perception of stop consonants have attracted a good deal of attention since speech synthesizers were built (Cooper et al., 1951). The cue which enables plosives to be distinguished from phonemes in other classes is probably the period of silence followed by the burst of energy at the moment of release.

The main cue which enables the voiced stops /b,d,g/ to be distinguished from the voiceless stops /p,t,k/ appears to be "voice onset time" or VOT (Liberman et al., 1958; Lisker and Abramson, 1967). VOT is the time between the release of the closure and the instant when the larynx begins vibrating. In voiced stops the larynx vibrations begin at, or even before, the instant of release whereas in voiceless stops there is a delay of some 50 msec. In some instances of voiced stops the larynx continues to vibrate during the period of closure. This shows up on a sonagram as a "voice bar".

Although VOT is, perhaps, the most important one for distinguishing voiced from voiceless stops, there are other acoustic cues. Lisker (1957a) succeeded in producing a series of stimuli differing only in the duration of closure which were perceived as "ruby" for short durations and "rupee" for long durations. With a closure duration of less than 75 msec the stop consonant was perceived as voiced, and with it greater than 130 msec the stop was heard as voiceless. More recently Haggard et al. (1970) have shown that for ambiguous stimuli a low rising fundamental frequency leads to the perception of an initial stop consonant as voiced, while a high falling fundamental leads to perception as voiceless.

The most important acoustic feature which enables the voiceless stop consonants to be distinguished from one another is the frequency of the noise burst at the moment of release (Liberman *et al.*, 1952). If the centre frequency of the burst is above 3 kHz a /t/ is perceived no matter which vowel follows. If the centre frequency is equal to or a little above the frequency of the second formant of the following vowel, a /k/ is heard. A /k/ may also be perceived with front vowels if the noise burst frequency is a little above the first formant frequency. With the burst at other frequencies (i.e. below the first formant frequency, between F1 and F2 for front vowels, or between F2 and 3 kHz for back vowels) a /p/ is usually heard.

The voiced stops are more complex. There is the period of closure, the burst, then formant transitions into the following vowel. It is the formant transitions which are probably the most important cues for the recognition of voiced plosives. Liberman *et al.* (1954) were the first to investigate the effect of formant transitions on the perception of voiced stops. They synthesized a number of two-formant vowels preceded by a rising first formant combined with various shapes of second formant as shown in Fig. 7.2. They found that a rising second formant was generally perceived as /b/, and a

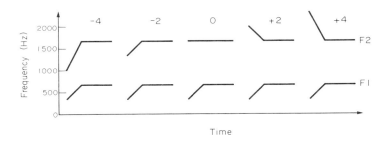

Fig. 7.2. Schematic spectrogram, showing the transitions of F2, of some of the stimuli used to produce /bɛ,dɛ,gɛ/.

falling one as /d/ or /g/. Before the front vowels the most rapidly falling transitions were heard as /g/ and the others as /d/, the extent of the transition being increased the more open the vowel (Fig. 7.3). For the back vowels the position was reversed: the rapidly falling transitions being perceived as /d/ and the more slowly falling ones as /g/.

Some generality can be introduced into the results by the "locus" concept. This is the place on the frequency scale at which the formant transition begins. Thus the first formant loci for all the stops are low. The second formant locus for /b/ is low, for /d/ it is high for back vowels and medium for front vowels, and for /g/ it is high for front vowels and medium for back vowels.

Harris *et al.* (1958) have investigated the loci for voiced stops followed by a three-formant vowel /æ/. They found that the second formant locus was low for /b/, medium for /d/ and high for /g/, while the third formant locus was low for /b/ and /g/ but high for /d/.

Although the burst is much briefer in voiced stops than in voiceless stops (it may be absent in a /b/) its position, nevertheless, contributes towards the perception of the

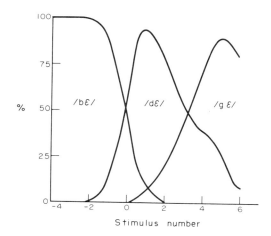

Fig. 7.3. Per cent of /b/, /d/ and /g/ responses as a function of F2 transition (data from Liberman *et al.*, 1954).

consonant (Hoffman, 1958). In certain syllables, where the formant transitions are minimal, the burst becomes the main cue for identifying the consonant (Ainsworth, 1968b). In the syllable /di/, for example, the second and third formant loci almost coincide with the formant frequencies of the vowel, so there are no formant transitions. If the syllable is preceded immediately by a short noise burst of high frequency, the syllable is unambiguously identified as /di/.

Most of the experiments with synthesized stimuli have been performed with initial stop consonants. Wang (1959) has investigated the perception of final plosives. He used a different technique. Recordings were made of natural speech, then the part containing the stop consonant was cut away from the rest and spliced on the end of a different syllable. In this way he was able to find out if any of the cues for the final consonant were contained in the preceding vowel (or consonant, in the case of a consonant cluster). This is important because final plosives before terminal junctures are not always released in connected speech. Wang found that the releases were additional cues for identifying all of the plosives, but the voiceless releases were the more helpful. This suggests that more cues for final voiced stops are contained within the vowel part of the syllable.

Fourcin (1968) has shown that adaptation to the voice which is speaking, which occurs with vowels (Broadbent and Ladefoged, 1960), also occurs with stop consonants. He used stimuli consisting of the word "hello" spoken by a man or a child followed by a synthesized stop consonant. The synthesized consonants were whispered so that no cues could be obtained from the pitch of the voice. Fourcin found that the listeners' judgements about the positions of the loci, as deduced from identification responses, depended on the speaker of the precursor.

In the time domain there seems to be a parallel process of adaptation to rate of speaking. Summerfield and Haggard (1972) found that the VOT boundary between voiced and voiceless stops depends on the syllabic rate of a carrier phrase and on the duration of the syllable in which the stop consonant occurs. Ainsworth (1973a) found that different durations of noise were required to synthesize /di/, /ti/ and /si/ depending on the duration of the vowel /i/.

Perception of nasals

Nasal sounds are probably distinguished from other speech sounds by the presence of a strong formant at about 200 Hz and relatively weak formants in the rest of their spectra. The nasals might be discriminated from one another by the positions of the poles and zeros in the steady part of the sound, or they might be distinguished by the formant transitions of the context vowel which result from the closing or opening of the oral tract.

Liberman *et al.* (1954) investigated the effect of formant transitions using stimuli generated by pattern-playback. They found that for vowel-nasal syllables a falling second formant transition produced an /m/ sound. A rising second formant was normally perceived as /n/, but the results with front vowels were unclear. Some /ŋ/ responses were also obtained with rising transitions.

Nakata (1959) has reported that for initial nasals the second formant locus is relatively low (800 to 1300 Hz) when the consonant is identified as /m/, somewhat higher (in the range 1500 to 2000 Hz) when the consonant is identified as /n/, and even higher (2000 to 2500 Hz) when the consonant is identified as /ŋ/. The lower limits apply when the adjacent vowel is /u/ and the upper limits when it is /i/.

The temporal course of nasal-vowel syllables has been studied by Hecker (1962) using an articulatory synthesizer. He found that more acceptable syllables were generated when the change from a nasal to an oral configuration took place in 150 msec than in 50 msec.

Perception of fricatives

Hughes and Halle (1956) and Strevens (1960) have investigated the spectral properties of fricative consonants. There are two cues which might conceivably be employed for distinguishing amongst them: the spectrum of the fricative part, and the transitions of the formants in the adjacent voiced part. The relative contributions of these cues have been investigated by Harris (1958) using the tape-splicing technique. She separated the fricative part from the voiced part of naturally produced syllables formed by the combination of /s,ʃ,f,θ/ with the vowels /i,e,o,u/. All possible combinations of fricative and voiced parts were spliced together. It was found that identification of /s/ and /ʃ/ was based mainly on the fricative part of the consonant, whereas identification of /f/ and /θ/ depended more on the voiced transitions. The experiment was repeated with the voiced fricatives and similar results were obtained; /z/ and /ʒ/ being most consistently identified by the fricative part, and /v/ and /ð/ by the voiced transition.

Although no formal perception experiments have been reported, the voiced fricatives are almost certainly distinguished from their voiced counterparts by the presence of energy in the low-frequency part of the spectrum. In some final voiced fricatives there is very little voicing, and in such cases their shorter duration might be employed to distinguish them from the voiceless fricatives. Another possibility is that the decision might be guided by linguistic rules with reference to the preceding phoneme.

Heinz and Stevens (1961) have shown that the spectra of fricatives contain zeros as well as poles. They synthesized a number of stimuli by means of noise excitation of a filter having one pole, and one zero whose frequency was an octave below that of the pole. They found that when the frequency of the pole was 2 to 3 kHz listeners heard /ʃ/, when it was 3 to 6 kHz they heard /s/, and from 7 to 8 kHz /f/ or /θ/. They were unable to distinguish consistently between /f/ and /θ/.

The experiment was repeated with the fricative followed by a synthesized vowel, /ɑ/, to form a syllable. Formant transitions joined the consonant to the vowel. The locus of the first formant was kept constant at 200 Hz and the locus of the second formant was varied throughout its range. When the intensity of the fricative part of the syllable was only 5 dB less than that of the vowel only /ʃ/ and /s/ were heard, the boundary between them occurring when the pole of the fricative filter was about 3 kHz. When the intensity of the fricative part was reduced to 25 dB below the vowel, /f/ and /θ/ were also heard. /ʃ/ was perceived most often with the pole at about 2.5 kHz, /s/ with it at 3.5 kHz, and /f/ and /θ/ with it at about 8 kHz. When the locus of the second formant was low (below 1 kHz) /f/ was heard most often, and when it was high (above 1.5 kHz) /θ/ was perceived.

Categorical perception

It has been observed in some experiments on the perception of synthesized consonants, when one of the parameters is varied throughout its range, the responses are nearly all in one category until the parameter reaches a certain value, then the proportion of responses changes rather rapidly until they are nearly all in another category. For example, in Fig. 7.3 when the locus of the second formant was below 1500 Hz mostly /b/ responses were obtained, between 1500 and 2000 Hz mostly /d/ responses, and above 2000 Hz mostly /g/ responses. The point at which the stimulus is perceived as changing from one category to another may be termed the "phoneme boundary".

The usefulness of this concept of phoneme boundary has been demonstrated in a number of experiments. Liberman *et al.* (1957) presented a number of synthesized syllables with a range of F2 loci to a group of listeners for identification as /b/, /d/ or /g/. A typical set of results is shown in Fig. 7.3 where the phoneme boundaries are clearly shown.

Liberman *et al.* then presented the same set of stimuli to the listeners for discrimination using the ABX paradigm. A is one of stimuli, B is the next stimulus, and X is the same as either A or B. The listeners are not asked to identify the sounds, but merely to say whether X is more like A or B. This paradigm for determining discriminability can obviously be applied to any sounds, and is not limited to speech sounds.

If the number of times when the category of X was chosen correctly is plotted against the number of the stimulus in the series, a discrimination function results. If A and B sound the same it will be impossible to tell whether X was the same stimulus as A or B, so this function will have a value of 50 per cent. On the other hand, if A and B are clearly identifiable, it will be easy to tell the category of X, and the value of the function will be 100 per cent.

A typical discrimination function obtained from listeners' responses is shown in Fig. 7.4. The regions of increased discriminability occur at the phoneme boundaries.

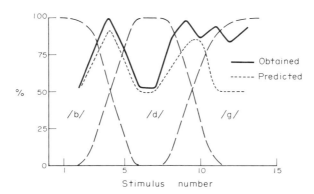

Fig. 7.4. Comparison of identification and discrimination of synthesized syllables (data from Liberman *et al.*, 1957).

Liberman *et al.* (1957) hypothesized that listeners are only able to distinguish one stimulus from another if the stimuli are of different phonemic categories. Thus stimuli numbers 1 and 2 would both be labelled /b/ by the listener and could not be distinguished, whereas stimuli 3 and 4 (which acoustically are just as dissimilar as 1 and 2) could be distinguished because 3 would be recognized as /b/ and 4 as /d/.

If p_n (b) is the probability of identifying stimulus n as /b/, p_n (d) the probability of identifying it as /d/, and p_n (g) the probability of identifying it as /g/, then the value of the discrimination function is given by (Liberman *et al.*, 1957):

$$D(n) = \tfrac{1}{2} + \tfrac{1}{4}[(p_n \text{ (b)} - p_{n+1} \text{ (b)})^2 + (p_n \text{ (d)} - p_{n+1} \text{ (d)})^2 + p_n \text{ (g)} + p_{n+1} \text{ (g)})^2].$$

The values of p_n (b), etc., can be obtained from the identification experiment, so the discrimination function can be calculated.

In the experiments of Liberman *et al.* it was found that when stimulus B differed from stimulus A by only one step in the series, little enhanced discrimination was observed or expected, as the step size was smaller than the span of the boundary. When stimulus B was two steps different from A, good agreement was obtained between the observed and calculated discrimination functions. With three steps between A and B, the acoustic difference was so great that the observed discrimination was nearly always higher than the calculated one.

Further evidence that enhanced discrimination of speech-like sounds is due to phonemic categorization has been obtained by Ainsworth (1974d). A series of sounds were synthesized consisting of a burst of noise followed by a vowel. These were categorized by listeners as /di/, /ti/ or /si/ depending on the duration of the noise burst. The positions of the phoneme boundaries were found to depend on the duration of the vowel /i/. Two identification experiments were performed with long (320 msec) and short (80 msec) vowels, and the positions of the phoneme boundaries were determined. Discrimination experiments were then performed, and it was found that the regions of enhanced discrimination followed the phoneme boundaries and also depended on the duration of the vowel in the syllable.

The positions of the phoneme boundaries depend on the linguistic background of the listener. Miyawaki *et al.* (1975) synthesized a series of syllables which changed from /r/ at one end to /l/ at the other. Discrimination tests with American listeners showed enhanced discrimination in the region of the phoneme boundary. With Japanese listeners, however, the discrimination function was flat. With Japanese listeners who had been brought up in America, the results were similar to those obtained with American listeners.

It was thought at one time that although consonant perception was categorical, vowel perception was not. Fry *et al.* (1962) synthesized a series of vowels which contained /ɪ/, /ɛ/ and /æ/. They obtained phoneme boundaries from an identification experiment, but failed to find any regions of enhanced discrimination. Fujisaki and Kawashima (1971), however, obtained clear peaks in the discrimination function of /i/ and /e/, and Stevens (1968) has found that a discrimination function with peaks was produced with vowels in a /bVl/ context.

It is possible that the stimuli used by Fry *et al.* differed from each other by too great an amount for the differential discriminability at phoneme boundaries to show up. The mean difference between one of their stimuli and the next was about 45 Hz in F1 and 20 Hz in F2. Flanagan (1955) found the difference limens for vowels was of the order of 4 per cent of the formant frequency, about 20 Hz for F1 and 60 Hz for F2. The series /ɪ, ɛ,æ/ are all front vowels, so are probably distinguished from one another by the frequency of F1. The stimuli differed sufficiently in this dimension for successive pairs to be discriminated. In the experiments of Fujisaki and Kawashima on the other hand, successive stimuli differed by only 10 Hz in F1 and 20 Hz in F2. With A and B two steps apart the stimuli spanned the phoneme boundary yet were insufficiently different to be discriminated if they fell into the same phonemic category. It thus appears that vowels are categorically perceived in the sense that enhanced discrimination is shown at phoneme boundaries, yet their discriminability is sufficiently acute for vowel sounds within a phonemic category to be distinguished.

Fujisaki and Kawashima (1971) have proposed a model to account for the results of their experiments. The principle is shown in Fig. 7.5. A sound is perceived and stored in

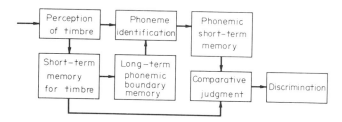

Fig. 7.5. The model of Fujisaki and Kawashima for the process of discriminating speech sounds.

a short-term auditory memory. A phoneme identification is also made, and the result stored in a short-term phonemic memory. When more stimuli are perceived, the judgement is made in terms of both their auditory images and their phonemic categorizations. The discrimination depends upon the result of both of these judgements.

Pisoni (1973) has obtained empirical evidence which supports the notion of two distinct memories. He measured discrimination functions for both stop consonants and vowels using the AB paradigm. (In this the listener hears two stimuli and is required to state whether they are the same or different.) Pisoni varied the interval between A and B. He found that for synthetic vowels the accuracy of discrimination was reduced as this interval was increased. For stop consonants, however, discrimination remained relatively stable despite the changes in this interval. The suggestion is that the enhanced discrimination of vowels depends upon their retention in the short-term auditory memory, the decay time of which is of the same order as the interval between the stimuli. In the phonemic memory, only categories are stored, and this is inherently more stable.

Consonant confusions

Miller and Nicely (1954) have examined the perceptual confusions which occur when nonsense syllables are heard in the presence of random noise and after band-pass filtering. The syllables consisted of the sixteen phonemes /p,t,k,f,θ,s,ʃ,b,d,g,v,ð,z,ʒ,m,n/ combined with the vowel /ɑ/. They analysed their results in terms of five linguistic features which can be used to distinguish these consonants. The features were:

1. *Voicing.* In /b,d,g,v,ð,z,ʒ,m,n/ the vocal cords vibrate, whereas in /p,t,k,f,θ,s,ʃ/ they do not. The first set have a periodic acoustic structure, but the second set have a noisy structure.
2. *Nasality.* The phonemes /m,n/ contain a nasal resonance, whereas the others do not.
3. *Affriction.* In /b,d,g,p,t,k,m,n/ the oral tract is closed, whilst in /f,θ,s,ʃ,v,ð,z,ʒ/ there is a constriction through which there is a turbulent flow of air.
4. *Duration.* The phonemes /s,ʃ,z,ʒ/ have a longer duration than the others. They also contain intense, high-frequency noise.
5. *Place.* This feature describes the position of the major constriction of the vocal tract. The phonemes /p,b,f,v,m/ are classed as front, /t,d,θ,s,ð,z,n/ as middle, and /k,g,ʃ,ʒ/ as back.

The results showed that voicing and nasality are much less affected by added noise than the other features. Affrication and duration were both affected by added noise, but were less affected than was place. Low-pass filtering affected the perception of the features in a similar way to the addition of noise, but high-pass filtering affected all features equally.

The features used by Miller and Nicely to explain the consonant confusions were chosen somewhat arbitrarily to conform with traditional linguistic features and those of articulatory phonetics. Alternatively the results of experiments in which consonant confusions are measured can be used to estimate the features which are extracted by the perceptual mechanism. The method is to use multidimensional scaling to determine the least number of dimensions which can explain the confusions. These dimensions are then associated with appropriate features. The variations of the method and the data employed have led to several perceptual feature systems which have been reviewed by Singh (1974). From his own studies Singh concludes that the perceptual features of consonants are nasality, voicing, sibilant, continuant, place and sonorant.

Adaptation

In the visual systems of many animals neurones have been found which do not respond to uniform fields of light but do respond to features of patterns such as edges and corners (Lettvin *et al.*, 1959; Hubel and Wiesel, 1962). Similarly in the auditory cortex of cats neurones have been found which respond only to the onset of tones or to rising tones (Evans and Whitfield, 1964). Such neurones are termed "feature detectors". Eimas and Corbit (1973) have suggested that there may be such feature detectors in the human auditory cortex which respond to linguistic features such as voicing or nasality. These detectors would form a useful part of a speech recognition system.

One of the properties of cortical neurones is that they habituate. They respond vigorously at first to an appropriate stimulus, but if the stimulus is repeated they respond less and less often. Eimas and Corbit suggest that this process of adaptation may also occur to the linguistic feature detectors in the human brain. They propose the existence of a pair of detectors, one of which responds to voiced sounds and one to voiceless sounds. They hypothesize that if one of these is overstimulated it will become fatigued. In this state the "voiced" detector will be less likely to respond to voiced sounds than it would otherwise be. Consequently if the position of the phoneme boundary between a pair of voiced and voiceless phonemes is measured with the voicing detector fatigued, a shift of the phoneme boundary towards the voiced phoneme will be observed.

Eimas and Corbit synthesized a series of stop-vowel syllables in which the VOT was varied so that a voiced stop occurred at one end of the series and its voiceless counterpart at the other. They repeated the voiced stop 75 times followed by one of the syllables in the series. This procedure was repeated until each of the syllables in the series had been tested several times. The position of the phoneme boundary was then compared with its position in the unadapted state. As expected, it was found that when the voiced stop /b/ was the adapter the boundary shifted to the /b/ end of the series, and when the voiceless stop /p/ was the adapter the boundary shifted in the other direction. Moreover, they found that these shifts could be produced by other adapters such as /d/ and /t/ even though the series of test sounds was /b/ to /p/. From these results they argue that it was the linguistic feature detectors for "voice" and "voiceless" which were being fatigued, rather than /b/- or /p/-phoneme detectors.

Bailey (1974) has suggested that it is the "cue" detectors rather than the linguistic feature detectors which were being fatigued. He points out that the hypothetical voicing detector is multi-cued, being triggered by formant transitions (Stevens and Klatt, 1971) and fundamental frequency contours (Haggard *et al.*, 1970) in appropriate situations, as well as by VOT.

A trimodal feature detector has been proposed by Cooper (1974) which reflects the place of articulation of a speech sound. Cooper employed a series of stop-vowel syllables in which the place of articulation of the stop consonant was cued by formant transitions. He found adaptation effects as expected. Bailey (1974), however, found that adaptation effects occur only if the adapter and the test syllables contain energy in the same region of the spectrum. This supports his contention that it is the cue detectors which are adapted, not the linguistic feature detectors.

In his first series of experiments Bailey (1973) found that with the two series

/bɑ/–/dɑ/ and /bɛ/–/dɛ/ the shift encountered in the cross-series condition was reduced compared with the within-series condition. Furthermore, with the series /bu/–/du/ and /bi/–/di/ where the spectral separation of the second formants in the two series is great, he found no adaptation in the cross-series condition.

In his next series of experiments, Bailey (1974) employed two series of stimuli /bɑ/–/dɑ/, one of which (series 1) contained a fixed second formant and a variable third formant locus, and the other of which (series 2) contained no third formant but had a variable second formant locus. With the adapter stimuli taken from series 2 and the test stimuli from series 1, the expected adaptation occurred; but with the adapter from series 1 and the test from series 2, there was no adaptation. In a subsidiary experiment, one series contained a fixed F2 and a variable F3, and the other a variable F2 and a fixed F3. With these stimuli adaptation was produced with both cross-series conditions. As the adapters were clear examples of /b/ or /d/ in every case, it seems unlikely that "place" detectors were adapted, and much more likely that cue detectors, triggered by relatively local formant transitions, were fatigued.

Further evidence in support of "cue" adaptation has been obtained by Ainsworth (1975). The phoneme boundary between /bɑ/ and /dɑ/ can be shifted towards /bɑ/ by means of /tɑ/ syllables, each consisting of a burst of noise followed by appropriate formant transitions. If the transitions are eliminated the syllable is still identified as /tɑ/, yet it will not cause the phoneme boundary to shift as far from its unadapted position.

Hemispheric specialization

There is some evidence that part of the left hemisphere of the brain is specialized to deal with language and speech-like sounds, leaving the right hemisphere to cope with other noises. Kimura (1961) noticed that patients with temporal lobe damage on the left had language difficulties, while those with brain damage on the right did not. Broadbent and Gregory (1964) found that the accuracy of recognition of spoken digits presented to the right ear (which is connected to the left auditory cortex) was greater than that of those presented to the left ear. On the other hand, Kimura (1964) found the opposite to be the case when melodies were presented to different ears.

In order to determine whether this specialization applies to low-level processing, such as phoneme recognition, or only at higher levels of processing, Shankweiler and Studdert-Kennedy (1967) presented dichotically pairs of syllables containing stop consonants, and isolated vowels. The listeners were asked to identify the sounds presented to each ear. It was discovered that stop consonants presented to the right ear were identified more accurately than those presented to the left. This phenomenon has become known as the right ear advantage (REA). The difference in accuracy of recognition of isolated vowel sounds in the two ears was found not to be statistically significant.

Studdert-Kennedy and Shankweiler (1970) repeated their experiments with naturally produced syllables and vowels, and obtained similar results. In this experiment they included final stop consonants, and found a significant, though reduced, REA.

They analysed the pattern of results produced by their listeners. Errors could occur in two ways: either they could arise by chance, or the signal in one ear could influence the signal in the other. In the first case the pattern of errors would be random, while in the second there would be blend errors (the signals combining before the phonetic features are extracted so that acoustic cues from one ear combine with those from the other ear to produce the error). It was found that there were many more of these "blend" errors than would be expected to arise by chance.

A theoretical explanation of the occurrence of REA for some speech sounds has been put forward by Liberman *et al.* (1967). The acoustic manifestation of many phonemes depends upon the context. For example, the second formant of /d/ in the syllable /di/ has a rising transition, whereas in /du/ it has a falling one. A speech recognizer which takes no account of the vowel in the syllable cannot be expected to realize that a rising and a falling transition are cues for the same phoneme. It will fail to recognize some of these "encoded" phonemes. Liberman *et al.* argue that the special "decoders" necessary for dealing with these phonemes are situated in the left hemisphere, so it is only with "encoded" speech sound that REA can be demonstrated.

Darwin (1971) has investigated the perception of fricative-vowel syllables presented dichotically. He found a right ear advantage. When the formant transitions between the fricative and vowel parts of the syllable were removed, the REA was much reduced. This was also true if the vowel part were removed entirely. If the fricative part were removed and the transitions were left intact, however, the REA remained. The importance of formant transitions has been confirmed by Haggard (1971), who found that REA also occurs with semivowels. Cutting (1972), however, reports REA with semivowels in initial but not in final position.

The results with vowels presented dichotically are somewhat complex. If the pitch and the formant frequencies of the vowels are such that the vowel sounds in the separate ears appear to have been produced by different speakers, REA occurs (Haggard, 1971). This advantage happens even if vowels have the same pitch, but appear to have been produced by different sizes of vocal tract, are mixed together in the same experiment (Darwin, 1971). If all the vowels appear to have been produced by the same voice, no REA occurs. This has been interpreted by Haggard (1971) to suggest that the special "decoders" located in the left hemisphere are required if the complexity of the perceptual task is great enough.

A curious effect with dichotically presented speech sounds has been reported by Studdert-Kennedy *et al.* (1970), Porter (1971) and others. This is the "lag" effect. If stop-vowel syllables are presented to the two ears asynchronously, performance with the lagging stimulus improves with increase in asynchrony, reaching an asymptote by 60 msec or so. Performance with the leading stimulus, on the other hand, tends to be as low, or lower, than at simultaneous presentation, and only begins to climb towards its asymptotic value after reaching a minimum at around 45 msec. For equivalent offset values the performance with the lagging signal almost always exceeds that of the leading signal.

One possible explanation of this phenomenon is that the lagging signal adds confusing information which interferes with the decision about the identity of the leading signal (Kirstein, 1973). In order to account for the delay of 30 to 50 msec which causes the maximum disruption, it is necessary to assume that the greatest interference occurs when the additional information from the second ear arrives at the moment when the decision about the identity of the consonant is about to be made (Porter, 1974).

There is some evidence that the central mechanism which decodes the signals from the two ears has a limited information capacity which can be exceeded when different signals arrive from two ears simultaneously. In monaural perception, if the intensity or bandwidth is reduced or if noise is added to the signal, the performance is reduced. In dichotic presentations, if any of these distortions are applied to the signal in one ear, the performance with that ear deteriorates as expected. The performance with the other ear, however, increases so that the total recognition score from the two ears remains almost constant (Cullen *et al.*, 1974). This behaviour is much the same regardless of whether the distortion is applied to the signal in the left ear or the signal in the right ear. To date, only experiments with stop vowel syllables have been carried out. It is not known whether the effect will occur with isolated vowels and other speech sounds.

In order to attempt to find out which parts of the brain are involved in decoding speech signals, Berlin *et al.* (1974) have performed dichotic listening tests with patients who have had parts of their brain removed. With temporal lobectomy patients they found that there was no lag effect, and that the "strong" (ipsilateral) ear continually out performed the "weak" (contralateral) ear, even with an asynchrony of 90 msec. With hemispherectomy patients there was, again, no lag effect, but also no interference. The "strong" ear functions at virtually 100 per cent. Berlin *et al.* note the similarity of the results between hemispherectomy patients, and normals in which the signal in one ear is distorted with added noise.

Bilateral adaptation

In order to determine the location of the detectors which are adapted by repeated syllables, Eimas *et al.* (1973) performed an experiment in which the adapter syllables were presented to one ear and the test syllables to the other ear. Using the /d/–/t/ series of stimuli, they found that shifts in the boundary could be obtained which were of the same order of magnitude as when the adapter and test syllables were presented to the same ear. This suggested that the detectors are located centrally rather than peripherally.

The next question is whether these detectors are part of the specialized speech recognizing mechanism, or part of the general auditory analysing equipment. Eimas *et al.* (1973) gated the /dɑ/ syllable so that only the first 50 msec were heard. This was not perceived as speech by any of their listeners. They repeated their experiment using this truncated stimulus as the adapter and the /dɑ/–/tɑ/ series as test syllables. No shifts in phoneme boundaries were found, suggesting that the detectors are part of the specialized speech recognizing mechanism.

Ades (1974) has shown that "peripheral" adaptation, as well as central, can take place. He employed a bilateral adaptation technique in which one ear was adapted with /bæ/ syllables and the other with /dæ/ syllables simultaneously. Boundary shifts were found in both ears in the direction of the adapting syllable. Ades has also confirmed that interaural transfer takes place when adapter and test syllables are applied to different ears.

In order to measure the amount of central adaptation and the amount of peripheral adaptation Ades performed another experiment in which the first formant of a syllable was presented to one ear, and the second and third formants were presented to the other. In one experiment these components were presented simultaneously so that binaural fusion took place, and in another experiment they were presented out of phase. It was found that adaptation occurred with both kinds of stimuli, but it was greater with the fused stimuli. Ades argues that the results with the "out of phase" stimuli represent the peripheral component of adaptation, and the additional adaptation with the fused stimuli represents the central component.

Ades (1974) proposes two models for his results. In one there are two peripheral sites of adaptation with pathways to a common central site (Fig. 7.6a), whilst in the other there are two sites which receive inputs from both ears (Fig. 7.6b), the stronger input being from the contralateral ear. Either model can explain the results at present. The conclusion, however, is that detectors which show adaptation effects appear to be located in both hemispheres of the brain.

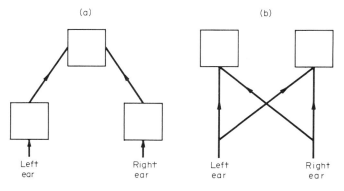

Fig. 7.6. Two possible models of the adaptation process.

CHAPTER 8

Perception of Prosodic Features

Although much of the message in speech is conveyed by the segmental phonemes, additional informant is carried by the prosodic features: stress, rhythm, and intonation. The noun "subject" and the verb "subject" are both represented by the phonemic string /sʌbdʒɛkt/, although the first syllable is stressed when the word is a noun and the second syllable is stressed when the word is a verb. Some of the rules governing the placement of stress in English are given by Chomsky and Halle (1968). In a similar way the statement "He is" and the question "He is?" are both represented by /hiːz/, although the meaning is very different in the two cases. This difference is encoded in the utterance by means of the intonation contour.

The physical parameters of the speech wave which signal the prosody of an utterance are the durations and intensities of the syllables, and the excursions of the fundamental frequency.

Perception of fundamental frequency

The difference limen for the fundamental frequency of vowel sounds has been measured by Flanagan and Saslow (1958). They found a DL of 0.3 to 0.5 Hz when the fundamental was of the order of 120 Hz. This is very similar to the DL of pure tones of this frequency as found by Nordmark (1968).

Askenfelt (1973) has measured the DLs of low-pass filtered pulse trains (which approximate the spectral characteristics of back vowels) and pure tones. He obtained values close to those of Nordmark, but found the DLs of pure tones were nearly twice as great as those of complex tones.

Perception of duration

There are certain pairs of phonemes which have identical spectral energy content but which differ from each other in duration. These may be employed to measure the accuracy with which the duration of various speech sounds are perceived. Fujisaki *et al.* (1975) have performed these measurements for Japanese.

They synthesized a number of pairs of words which were identical except that one contained the "short" phoneme and one the "long". For example, (ise) "a place name" and (isse) "a unit of area". They also synthesized a series of intermediate words containing intermediate values of the duration of the relevant phoneme. Listeners were asked to identify each of the stimuli as one of the words at the extreme of the series. Curves were obtained of the probability of identifying a stimulus as one of the words as a function of the duration of the relevant phoneme. The duration which gave 50 per cent was the phoneme boundary, and the standard deviation of the points gave a measure of the accuracy of the perception of duration.

The phoneme boundaries and accuracies for a number of phonemes are shown in Table 8.1. If these are compared with the accuracies with which the durations of

Table 8.1. Phoneme boundaries and accuracy of identification of various synthetic Japanese contexts (Fujisaki et al., 1975)

Stimulus	Boundary (msec)		Accuracy (msec)	
	word	sentence	word	sentence
Vowel /oi/–/ooi/	156	168	9.5	7.1
Fricative /ise/–/isse/	166	165	16	10
Plosive /ita/–/itta/	169	164	11	8.9
Nasal /ama/–/amma/	141	152	10	8.5

various non-speech sounds are perceived (Chapter 3), it will be observed that durations are generally perceived more accurately for speech sounds. The accuracy with which a 160-msec vowel can be perceived is about 8 msec whereas the corresponding figure for a 500-Hz tone of the same length is about 12 msec. Similar figures obtain for nasal sounds. The duration of the silent interval of a plosive can be perceived with an accuracy of about 10 msec, yet a pause between two tones can be perceived with an accuracy of only 20 msec. The position is reversed for fricative sounds, however. There is a variability in the perceived phoneme boundary between "ise" and "isse" of 10–16 msec, but the corresponding accuracy with which "noise" stimuli can be discriminated is 7–9 msec.

Stress

In English there are at least two kinds of stress: "word stress" and "sentence stress". Word stress serves to distinguish between two meanings or uses of a word as mentioned in the illustrations in the introduction to this chapter. Sentence stress is used to indicate the most important word or words in a sentence or phrase.

Fry (1955) has investigated some of the physical correlates of word stress. He measured the duration and intensity of the vowels in a number of words, such as "permit" and "object" which may be used either as a noun (with the stress on the first syllable) or as a verb (with it on the second). He found, as was expected, that the syllable which had the longest duration and the greatest intensity was the syllable which listeners judged to be stressed. In order to discover which of these factors is perceptually the most important, he synthesized a number of words in which the duration and intensity of the vowels were varied independently. Listeners were asked to indicate which syllable was stressed. It was found that when the durations of both syllables were equal and the relative intensity varied throughout the range found in speech, the percentage of "noun" judgements increased from about 45 to 75 per cent. When the intensities of the vowels were equalized, and the relative durations varied throughout their range, however, the percentage changed from 20 to 90 per cent. It would appear, therefore, that although intensity and duration both contribute to the perception of stress, duration is the more important factor. In a later paper Fry (1958) investigated the possibility of fundamental frequency as a correlate of stress. He found that the syllable with the higher fundamental was perceived as stressed.

Rhythm and tempo

There are two prosodic features which describe the temporal characteristics of a spoken utterance: tempo and rhythm. Tempo is the rate at which the utterance is spoken. This varies from person to person and occasion to occasion. Some people habitually speak faster than others. A person delivering a public lecture will probably speak more slowly than he does in normal conversation, whereas a person commentating on a sporting event (other than a cricket match!) will speak more quickly.

The rhythm of an utterance is the pattern of time intervals which elapse between the occurrence of stressed syllables. There are at least three theories of rhythm: the "isochronous foot" model in which the intervals between stresses are always the same, the "comb" model in which the intervals between stresses are preprogrammed, but not necessarily equal, and the "chain" model in which each speech gesture is triggered by the completion of the previous one (Fig. 8.1).

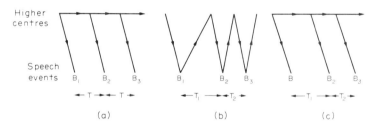

Fig. 8.1. Three models of speech rhythm (a) isochrony, (b) chain model and (c) comb model.

The "isochronous foot" model was proposed by Classe (1939) and has been developed by Abercrombie (1965). In a way analogous to the analysis of poetry, the utterance is divided into "feet" in such a way that the first syllable in each foot is a stressed syllable. If the model is correct the duration of every foot will be equal. Measurements by Uldall (1971) did not support this theory completely, but did suggest that there was a tendency towards isochrony. For one particular speaker Uldall found that the average duration of feet containing only one stressed syllable was 440 msec, whereas the average duration of three-syllable feet (one stressed plus two unstressed) was only 540 msec. As 50 msec is rather too short for an unstressed syllable, the stressed syallables in polysyllabic feet must be shortened. The average duration of four-syllabic feet, however, was found to be 760 msec. This suggests that the simple model breaks down for feet containing a large number of syllables.

Lennenberg (1967) has suggested a method for testing the isochrony hypothesis. The time intervals between several thousand successive releases of voiceless stops, or other detectable features associated with syllable onset, could be measured and a time-interval histogram produced. If the isochrony hypothesis were correct, a multi-modal distribution would result with the interval between the peaks giving the period of the underlying rhythm of the speech. This experiment has been performed by Ohala (1975), but no regular peaks in the time interval histogram were observed. This experiment only tests for isochrony at the syllable level, however, not at the level of linguistic stresses.

A method of testing whether the "comb" model or the "chain" model applies to speech was proposed by Kozhevnikov and Chistovich (1965). They suggested that a speaker repeat an utterance containing the events B_1, B_2 and B_3 a number of times, and that the intervals B_1B_2, B_2B_3, etc., be measured. There will be some variability in these intervals in successive repetitions of the utterance. In the case of the chain model the variability of each interval should be independent of each other interval so that the variance of a large interval, $V(B_1B_3)$, should equal the sum of the variances of the component intervals.

$$V(B_1B_3) = V(B_1B_2) + V(B_2B_3).$$

For the comb model, provided the tempo remains constant for successive repetitions, greater control will be exercised over the timing of longer portions of speech, so that

$$V(B_1B_3) < V(B_1B_2) + V(B_2B_3).$$

Kozhevnikov and Christovich found the latter relationship held for the speech material they analysed. The comb model is, thus, perhaps the best model for Russian speech, and this may well apply to other languages.

Duration of syllables

A possible model for the durations of syllables in words or phrases in Swedish has been proposed by Lindblom (1975). It was found that for sentences pronounced without junctures, and in a neutral manner, the longer the phrase the greater the amount of syllable shortening. In words occurring at the end of the sentence the syllables tended to be longer than in words at the beginning of the sentence, which in turn were slightly longer than those in the middle of the sentence. These effects can be described by the formula:

$$S = \frac{D}{(a+1)^\alpha + (b+1)^\beta}$$

where S is the duration of the syllable, D is the "intrinsic" duration of the syllable, a is the number of syllables which follow the syllable, b is the number of syllables which precede it, and α and β are consonants. By substituting appropriate values of D it was possible to compute syllable durations which corresponded quite well with the measured durations of syllables.

The formula above agrees with other published results. It predicts the shortening of syllables in polysyllabic feet as found by Uldall (1971) and it could form the basis of a comb model of speech timing similar to the one suggested to Kozhevnikov and Chistovich (1965).

An interesting suggestion has been made by Huggins (1975) concerning the range over which this syllable shortening effect occurs. He found that it crosses word boundaries but does not always effect all of the unstressed syllables to the next stressed syllable. He found that if a syntactic boundary, such as between a noun phrase and a verb phrase, intervened between two stressed syllables only those syllables to the left of this boundary were shortened.

Intonation

In some languages, the "tone" languages such as Mandarin Chinese, intonation is used to determine the lexical meaning of a word. Certain words which are represented by identical phonemic strings will have different meanings depending upon whether they are spoken with a rising or a falling pitch. In English, and most European languages, however, intonation is used to convey grammatical form.

The physical correlate of the intonation contour is fundamental frequency of the excitation source as a function of time. As the fundamentals of the voices of men, women and children cover different ranges of frequency, it is changes in frequency which are important, rather than absolute values. Jassem (1975) recorded an utterance spoken in seven different ways. Twenty listeners were asked to mimic these utterances, and their efforts were recorded. Pitch curves were obtained from these recordings. The frequency and range of each voice was then determined by constructing histograms. These two factors were employed to normalize the pitch curves, and good agreement was found between the normalized curves of each utterance for all of the speakers.

A theory of the use of intonation in English has been proposed by Halliday (1963). He suggests that any utterance can be divided into a series of "tone" groups. Each tone group consists of one or more "feet", and contains up to seven syllables. The most important syllable is known as the "tonic syllable". The tone group is divided into the "pretonic", the syllables which precede the tonic syllable, and the "tonic", the remainder of the tone group. The most important part of the intonation contour is the pitch change during the tonic. This follows one of the five courses shown in Fig. 8.2 if the tone group contains one tonic syllable, or one of the two courses shown if it

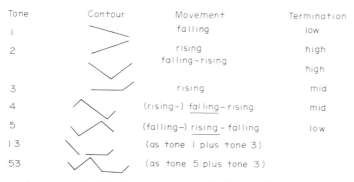

Fig. 8.2. The tone system of Halliday (1963).

contains two tonic syllables. The pitch movement in the pretonic may follow any of the paths shown in Fig. 8.3. The movement in the pretonic is somewhat constrained by tonic which it precedes.

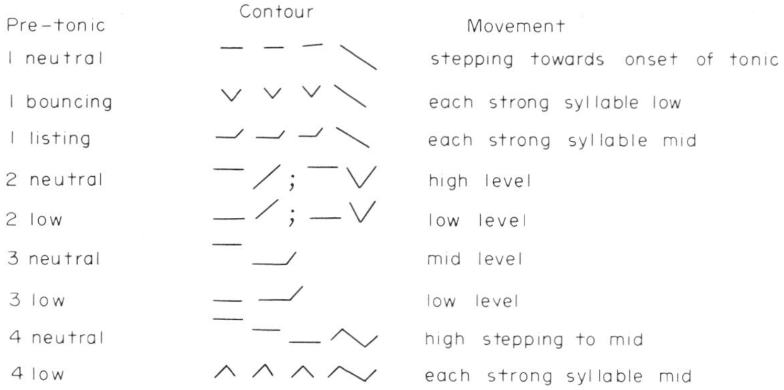

Fig. 8.3. Contours of the pre-tonics of the tone system of Halliday (1963).

The tone which is selected for a particular utterance is determined by the grammatical structure of the sentence. The tones are used in a contrastive way. Tone 1 (falling) is used for a neutral statement or answer, but tone 2 (rising) is employed if the statement or answer is contradictory. If, however, there is a reservation in the statement or answer, tone 4 (flat rising) is used. Tone 2 is also used for a question (unless it begins with a "wh" word). If a reply is non-commital, tone 3 is used, but if it is assertive the tone will be tone 5.

In reply to the question:

"Is it three feet long?" Tone 2.

The neutral reply would be "Yes, three feet". Tone 1.

The contradictory reply "Four feet". Tone 2.

The non-commital reply "Three feet, I don't know". Tone 3.

The reserved reply "Three feet, possibly". Tone 4.

The assertive reply "Three feet, definitely". Tone 5.

An alternative method of describing the intonation contour of sentences was developed by Pike (1945). He considers that any contour can be described in terms of four contour points. These are extra high, high, mid and low. The actual frequencies vary from individual to individual, and each individual varies his intervals from time to time. They are numbered in order with extra high represented by 1 and low by 4. Pike considers that four levels are just enough. With three it would not be possible to describe all the contours which are found, whereas five or six would leave many logical possibilities which are not utilized.

In this notation the examples above can be rewritten as:

Tone 1. Yes, three feet.

       2   4

Tone 2. Four feet.

       3   1

Tone 3. Three feet, I don't know.

      3   3   2

Tone 4. Three feet, possibly.

      3   4   4 3

Tone 5. Three feet, definitely.

      3   4   2   4

Thus the intonation contour of an utterance may be described. The mechanisms employed for perceiving the pitch of tones and complex sounds may be used in the perception of intonation contours, or some special mechanism specific to speech and language may be employed. Now that synthesis-by-rule systems are available which will generate good segmental phonemes, it is expected that research in this area will develop rapidly.

CHAPTER 9

Perception of Distorted Speech

There are a number of operations, which occur in natural circumstances or which may be introduced deliberately, which distort the speech wave, and thereby affect the recognition of the message. Some of the effects of these distortions on the perception of speech will be considered in this chapter.

Frequency distortions

The limits of hearing are approximately 20 Hz to 20,000 Hz, but the information-bearing features of speech lie in the region between 100 Hz and 12,000 Hz. A much narrower range, however, is adequate for speech communication. A typical telephone system transmits signals only in the 300-Hz to 3400-Hz range. A systematic study of the effects of limiting the frequency range has been carried out by French and Steinberg (1947). They employed high-pass and low-pass filters to limit the frequency ranges of nonsense syllables. The results they obtained are shown in Fig. 9.1. It will be seen that filtering out all the frequencies above 3400 Hz gives an intelligibility score of nearly 90 per cent for nonsense syllables. This is quite sufficient for error-free communication with continuous, meaningful speech.

It is interesting to note that either the range below 1900 Hz or above 1900 Hz gives

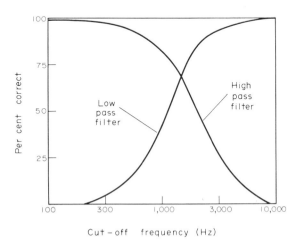

Fig. 9.1. Percent of syllables correctly identified as a function of cut-off frequency for low-pass and high-pass filtering.

96

an intelligibility score of about 67 per cent. Even this is sufficient to permit an easily intelligible conversation, so it would appear that no range of frequency is completely indispensable to the perception of speech.

Amplitude distortions

When an amplifier is overloaded the peak of the wave is clipped as shown in Fig. 9.2.

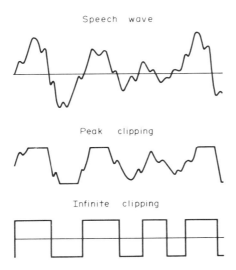

Fig. 9.2. Peak clipping of a speech wave.

Licklider (1946) measured the intelligibility of speech with peak-clipping in the range 0–20 dB, and found that it never fell below 96 per cent. Communication was essentially perfect. Between 20 and 50 dB, the intelligibility fell to about 70 per cent, but then remained constant even with infinite clipping. (Infinite clipping is the condition where the signal is rectangular in shape, but crosses the axis at the same points as the original speech wave as shown in Fig. 9.2.)

Licklider and Pollack (1948) investigated the perception of speech which had been distorted in various ways. They employed three operations: differentiation, integration, and infinite clipping. Differentiation is equivalent to tilting the frequency spectrum of the speech by +6 dB per octave so that the high-frequency components are amplified compared with the low-frequency components, and integration is equivalent to tilting the spectrum by −6 dB per octave. By combining the operations with infinite clipping, the ten distortions shown in Table 9.1 are produced.

Lists of phonetically balanced monosyllabic words (Egan, 1948) were employed as the speech material. The resulting intelligibility scores are shown in Table 9.1. No distortion, differentiation only, and integration only produced essentially 100 per cent intelligibility. Differentiation and clipping, and differentiation, clipping and integration produced only slightly less intelligibility, whereas clipping, clipping and integrating, and

Table 9.1. The effects of various combinations of differentiation, integration and infinite peak clipping on the intelligibility of speech (Licklider and Pollack, 1948)

Distortion	Intelligibility score (per cent)
No distortion	99
Differentiation	99
Integration	99
Differentiation and clipping	97
Differentiation, clipping and integrating	97
Clipping and integrating	70
Clipping	70
Clipping and differentiating	68
Integrating and clipping	17
Integrating, clipping and differentiating	17

clipping and differentiating produced somewhat worse results. Integrating and clipping, and integrating, clipping and differentiating produced very poor results.

The only information contained in a clipped-speech signal is the times of occurrence of the zero-crossings of the original wave, and the only information in a differentiated and clipped wave is the times of occurrence of the maxima and minima of the original wave. In order to investigate the importance of positive- and negative-going zero-crossings, and maxima and minima, Ainsworth (1967) produced signals which consisted of short pulses at just these instances. Positive- and negative-going zero-crossings, for example, were signalled by positive and negative pulses, or both by pulses of the same polarity. It was found that the polarity and shape of the signals was unimportant, but that transforms which maintained some distinction between the different kinds of zero-crossings were more intelligible. Furthermore, it was found that more information is contained in the time intervals between maxima and minima than between zero-crossing of the speech wave. Vowel-like sounds were less often confused than fricative-like ones.

If the axis of the speech wave is shifted (Fig. 9.3) and a clipped wave is produced at the new zero-crossings, the zero-crossings of the new wave differ from the zero-crossings of the original wave by small time intervals. If the axis is shifted by -50 dB of the amplitude of the original wave, the intelligibility is about 90 per cent, whereas a shift of -10 dB reduced the intelligibility to only 20 per cent (Tamaya and Hiramatu, 1958). Alternatively, if the zero-crossings of the clipped wave are delayed by random time intervals up to a maximum delay, the intelligibility drops from 100 per cent of the clipped-speech rate for maximum delays of 1 or 2 μsec down to about 30 per cent for maximum delays of 400 μsec (Tanaka and Okamoto, 1964).

Time distortions

If recorded speech is played back at a slower or faster rate than the one at which it was recorded, expansion or compression of the time scale results. Unfortunately the spectrum is contracted or expanded by the same factor so that the fundamental and formant frequencies of the speech are altered. It has been shown by Fletcher (1929) and

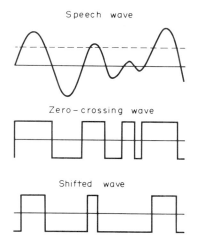

Fig. 9.3. Effect of shifting the zero before infinite clipping of a speech wave.

by Klumpp and Webster (1961) that intelligibility begins to deteriorate with speed changes in the ratio of 1.5:1.

Various devices have been produced which enable the time scale to be changed independently of the frequency scale. Fairbanks *et al.* (1954) describe a system in which a rotating head picks up a recorded signal from a magnetic tape loop. By altering the speed of the tape or the rotating head, the time scale or the frequency scale can be compressed or expanded. A modern device which performs the same function by digital techniques has been developed by Koch (1972). It has been found that speech can be understood if it is played back at a much greater speed than that at which it was spoken, provided that some such device is used to keep the spectrum constant.

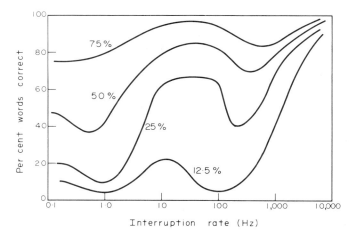

Fig. 9.4. Effect of interruption on the intelligibility of speech. The percentage of time the speech was on is shown (data from Miller and Licklider, 1950).

Another way in which the time scale can be distorted is by periodically interrupting the signal. The results of some experiments by Miller and Licklider (1950) are shown in Fig. 9.4. At an interruption rate of 0.1 Hz (once every 10 sec) each utterance (monosyllabic words were employed as the test material) was either heard or not, so if the speech is interrupted half of the time (50 per cent) the measured intelligibility will be 50 per cent. Between 1 and 10 Hz, some phonemes are missed completely in most words so the intelligibility falls. At 10 to 100 Hz enough features are heard for many syllables to be recognized. At 10 kHz the interruptions correspond to high-frequency modulation which does not reduce intelligibility.

Masking of speech

In a natural communication environment the listener hears other sounds at the same time as he hears speech. The other sounds may be other conversations, aeroplanes, sirens or even pneumatic drills. It is therefore useful to perform experiments which will enable the intelligibility of speech to be predicted in various situations. It has been found by Stevens *et al.* (1946) that pure tones have the greatest detrimental effect on intelligibility if they have a frequency of about 300 Hz if they are intense, and of about 500 Hz if they are weaker. This is what might have been expected from the results of masking one tone with another. In the case of speech the most intense component is the first formant.

The effects of white noise on speech intelligibility have been measured by Fletcher (1929). The speech signal needs to be about 25 dB above the threshold of hearing for it to be intelligible, so below this point the threshold for intelligibility is independent of noise level. Above this point, the intensity is raised in order to maintain intelligibility. In most practical situations the speech should be about 6 dB above the noise for satisfactory communication, although speech is detectable at an intensity of about 18 dB below the intensity of the noise.

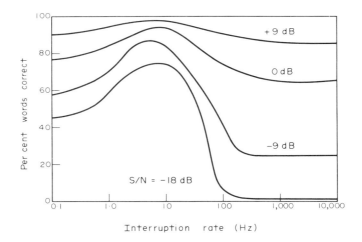

Fig. 9.5. Effect of noise interruption on the intelligibility of speech for various signal-to-noise ratios. The noise was on half the time, off half the time (data from Miller and Licklider, 1950).

In everyday situations noise is often not continuous, but is periodically interrupted. It is of interest, therefore, to measure the intelligibility of speech in such a situation. Miller and Licklider (1950) added to speech white noise which was gated so that it was present for only half of the time. They obtained the results shown in Fig. 9.5. If the interruption rate is greater than 100 times a second the noise is effectively continuous, and the intelligibility depends upon the signal-to-noise ratio. At ten times a second some of the syllables are heard and many of the others can be guessed, so the intelligibility score rises. At slower rates half of the words are heard and, if the noise is strong enough to mask the speech, half are missed so the intelligibility is about 50 per cent.

Effect of context

Another factor which influences the intelligibility of speech is context. Obviously if the number of words in the vocabulary is small and they are phonetically distinct from each other (for example, the ten digits) it is much less likely that errors of communication will occur than if the vocabulary is large and contains words which differ by only a single distinctive feature.

Miller *et al.* (1951) have measured the intelligibility of digits, words in sentences, and nonsense syllables as a function of signal-to-noise ratio. Their results are shown in Fig. 9.6. The digits are recognized perfectly with a signal-to-noise ratio of $-6\,dB$, whereas the words in sentences are not recognized perfectly until about $+18\,dB$. At this signal-to-noise ratio the nonsense syllables have an intelligibility of less than 70 per cent.

The effects of vocabulary size were examined in further detail. The same type of intelligibility tests were performed on monosyllabic word sets containing 2,4,8,16, 32,256 or an unspecified number of words. For the restricted vocabularies the listeners were informed of the alternatives. The results of the tests are shown in Fig. 9.7. It is clear that as the size of the vocabulary increases, the signal-to-noise ratio necessary to maintain a given level of performance also increases.

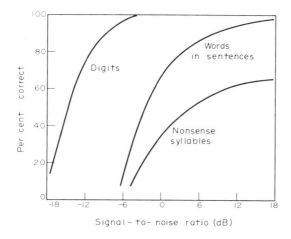

Fig. 9.6. Effects of context and signal-to-noise ratio on the intelligibility of speech.

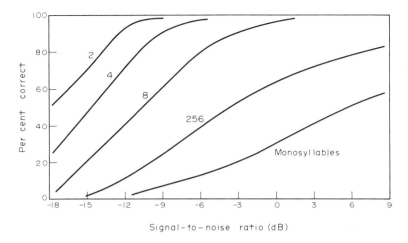

Fig. 9.7. Effects of size of vocabulary and signal-to-noise ratio on the intelligibility of speech.

Cocktail-party effect

When a number of conversations are being carried on simultaneously in the same room, it is normally possible to follow a selected conversation even though the total loudness of the other conversations seems greater. Cherry (1953) has performed some interesting experiments which clarify this ability.

Two messages, spoken by the same speaker, were recorded on magnetic tape. These were played back simultaneously to a listener who was asked to repeat one of the messages word by word or phrase by phrase. The listener found this task very difficult, but if he was allowed to replay the tape several times he got it right in the end. If the listener was allowed to write down parts of the message as he identified them, he completed the task much quicker.

In the second series of tests the two messages were played simultaneously to the two separate ears of the listener. The listener was then easily able to repeat the message in one of his ears, but at the end he could remember nothing of the message in the other ear. Subsequent experiments showed that if the language of the message in the unattended ear changed from English to German, the listener was unaware of the fact. The same result was obtained if the message in the second ear was played backwards so that it was meaningless. It was only if the speaker of the message changed from male to female, or if a steady tone was substituted, that the listener noticed that the signal in the unattended ear had changed.

Cherry explains these results in terms of a statistical filter. Provided that the signal in the unattended ear has the same statistical properties, as has German spoken by the same voice or the voice played backwards, the message will be filtered out and ignored. If the statistical pattern changes, however, conscious perception is interrupted with this information.

Verbal transformation effect

When a word, or a phrase, is repeated over and over again the perceived word occasionally suddenly changes. For example, Warren (1961) found that when the phrase "lame-duck" was repeated with a tape loop, the following phrases were perceived:

duckling, acclaimed, claim-duck, claim-de,
dark-claim, claim-dock, dock-lane, ducklin,
came-dark, claimed, duck-lame, I claimed.

Warren reports that when a single word is repeated at a rate of twice a second for 3 min, the average young adult hears about thirty changes involving about six different forms.

There are some remarkable effects of age of the listener on the frequency of verbal transformation. Children of the age of 5 experience either very few or no verbal transformations. At 6, half of the children tested heard transformations, and at the age of 8 all children appear to hear them. The rate of changes apparently remains approximately constant into the 20s, and then declines gradually. For listeners over 65 the rate has been found to be only a fifth of the rate for young adults, and is approximately equal to the rate for 5 year olds. This is not due to any decrease in hearing acuity with age, as the older people report the words that were actually spoken more accurately than the young. Children often hear nonsense words which contain phonetic sequences which do not occur in English. Young adults occasionally report nonsense words, but they only contain permitted phonetic sequences. Older people, on the other hand, report only meaningful words.

The mechanism responsible for the verbal transformation effect can only be guessed at. The shifting of phonetic boundaries by constant repetition is probably involved, and this possibly reflects the fatiguing of neurones. Substitution of neighbouring phonetic elements ("sea shore" for "see-saw") is a common transformation. Other mechanisms, however, must be involved to account for the variability with age of the listener.

Perception of temporal order

When a sequence of four sounds (a high-frequency tone, a buzz, a low-frequency tone, and a hiss) is repeated over and over again, listeners are unable to tell the order in which the sounds occur if the duration of each sound is less than or equal to 200 msec (Warren and Obusek, 1972). This is surprising since the average phoneme in speech lasts for only 70–80 msec, and listeners have no difficulty in determining the order in which phonemes occur in a word. When the tones, buzzes and hisses were replaced by vowel sounds cut out of the centres of sustained vowels, the listeners did no better in reporting the temporal order. When 50 msec of each vowel was erased, however (leaving vowels 150 msec in duration), some of the listeners were able to report the order correctly. When the vowel sounds were replaced by natural vowels of 150-msec duration with natural onsets and offsets, all of the listeners were able to tell the order in which the vowels occurred. These experiments give additional support to the hypothesis that speech perception is a special case of auditory perception, and that listeners have special abilities for dealing with speech-like sounds.

CHAPTER 10

Automatic Speech Recognition

An automatic speech recognizer may be defined as any mechanism, other than the human auditory system, which decodes the acoustic signal produced by the human voice into a sequence of linguistic units which contain the message that the speaker wishes to convey. This includes both the "phonetic typewriter", a hypothetical device which types any words spoken into it, and "speech understanding systems" (Newell *et al.*, 1971) which extract the intended meaning from the words and carry out some appropriate action such as replying to a question or controlling a robot.

Early speech recognizers

One of the first modern speech recognizers was built by Davis *et al.* (1952). A block diagram of their apparatus is shown in Fig. 10.1. It was intended to recognize spoken digits. The speech wave was first split into two bands by passing the wave through a 1000-Hz high-pass and a 800-Hz low-pass filter. The number of zero-crossings per second in each band was then counted, giving approximate measures of the frequencies

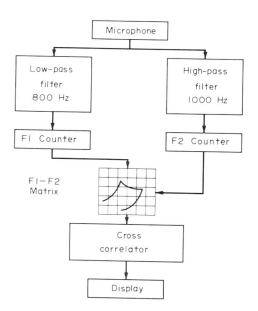

Fig. 10.1. The digit recognizer of Davis *et al.* (1952).

104

of the first and second formants. The first formant range (200–800 Hz) was quantized into six 100-Hz steps and the second formant range (500–2500 Hz) into five 500-Hz steps. A matrix with thirty elements representing the F1–F2 plane was thus produced. For a given spoken digit the time for which the F1–F2 trajectory occupied each element was determined.

A reference pattern was established for each digit. When a new digit was spoken, the pattern produced was cross-correlated with each of the reference patterns. This gave an approximate measure of the probability that a particular digit had been spoken, thus enabling the most likely digit to be chosen.

Provided that the reference patterns were adjusted for a particular speaker, the performance of the machine was quite encouraging. It is reported that it correctly recognized the digit spoken about 98 per cent of the time. When a new speaker used the machine, however, if no adjustments were made, the recognition score could be as low as 50 per cent.

In a later development of a similar system, Dudley and Balashek (1958) built a machine which performed a spectral analysis of the speech with a bank of band-pass filters 300 Hz wide. The output of the filter bank was cross-correlated with stored patterns, and the best match was selected as the spoken digit. This scheme also produced good results with the speaker who generated the stored patterns, but was less successful for other speakers.

In order to produce a more general purpose speech recognizer which would recognize phonemes rather than words, and so be able to deal with larger vocabularies, Wiren and Stubbs (1956) built a device which was based on the distinctive feature hypothesis. The principle of the device is outlined in Fig. 10.2. The "voiced" sounds were

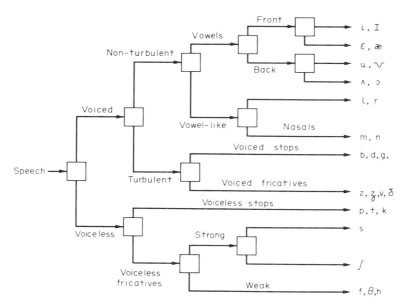

Fig. 10.2. The binary classification scheme of Wiren and Stubbs (1956).

first separated from the "voiceless" sounds, then the "voiceless" sounds were separated into fricatives and voiceless stops. Finally the strong and weak fricatives were separated from each other. In the "voiced" branch and turbulent sounds (voiced stops and voiced fricatives) were separated from the vowels and vowel-like sounds (nasals and glides). This principle of binary classification according to linguistic features can be repeated until a single phoneme is isolated.

Fairly good results were reported. With vowels in short words pronounced by twenty-one speakers an accuracy of 94 per cent was obtained. A system in which there were sufficient branches for every phoneme to be isolated was not, however, completely implemented.

A rather different attempt to use linguistic information was tried in a machine built by Fry and Denes (1958). They took advantage of the fact that the probability of one phoneme following another depends on the identity of the first phoneme. Their machine consisted of a spectrum analyser, a spectral-pattern matching system, and a store containing the probabilities of any phoneme following another in spoken English. The phoneme-recognition set comprised four vowels and nine consonants. The overall performance of the machine was not particularly good, but the use of the digram probabilities improved the word recognition accuracy from 24 per cent to 44 per cent.

Other forms of pre-processing

Each of the speech recognizers considered so far consisted of an acoustic analyser followed by a pattern classifier. The acoustic analyser generally produced some form of spectrum. As none of the machines achieved an accuracy of 100 per cent, it was thought for a while that perhaps this form of analysis was inappropriate. For this reason, and for reasons of economy, other forms of analysis were explored. Possibly because of its ease of implementation, zero-crossing analysis was popular. Sakai and Doshita (1962) reported a speech recognizer which was based partly on this kind of analysis. Zero-crossing measurements were combined with measures of the variations of energy in various frequency regions. It was claimed that the device correctly recognized 90 per cent of the vowels and 70 per cent of the consonants, although not all phonemes were allowed as input. Other speech-recognition devices which employed zero-crossing time-interval analysis were reported by Bezdel and Chandler (1965), Purton (1968), Lavington (1968) and Green (1971). Each of these showed promise, but none achieved useful recognition scores except by severe restrictions of vocabulary and speakers.

Another type of pre-processing was introduced by Teacher et al. (1967). Their recognition system was based on the premise that a single, dominant formant is the main acoustic feature responsible for the recognition of any particular phoneme. They termed this the single equivalent formant (SEF). This is shown in Fig. 10.3. For the back vowels the SEF is identical with F1 and for the front vowels it is near to F2, whilst for the middle vowels it lies between F1 and F2. The frequency of the SEF can be determined by picking the dominant peak in the spectrum after pre-emphasis of +6 to 9 dB per octave. Three parameters of the SEF (frequency, amplitude and manner of excitation) were measured, and used as data for a computer program which performed the recognition. With a vocabulary of 10 digits, an accuracy of 90 per cent was obtained with the ten speakers who had been used to train the device.

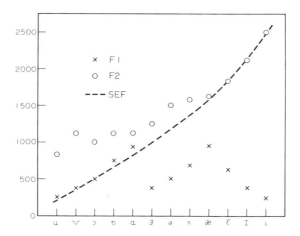

Fig. 10.3. Relationship between the single equivalent formant (SEF) and F1 and F2 for the vowels of English.

An interesting development in automatic speech recognizers was reported by Reddy (1967). Digital computers were finding increasing application in speech-recognition systems because of the ease with which the programs could be changed. In such systems Fourier analysis often accounts for a large proportion of the processing time [even if the FFT technique is employed (Cooley and Tukey, 1965)] so that in many systems a cruder form of frequency analysis, such as zero-crossing analysis, was employed. Such forms of analysis, however, lack the precision required for some of the discriminations required for speech recognition. In Reddy's system, zero-crossing analysis was used to segment the speech signal into portions corresponding approximately to phoneme units, then Fourier analysis was employed to make the necessary discriminations in the centres of the voiced regions. This was one of the first instances in which an attempt was made to employ the kind of analysis which was appropriate to the input signal.

Some problems

In spite of these ingenious methods of extracting the relevant parameters from speech signals, there seemed to be an upper limit of 90–95 per cent for a vocabulary of ten words spoken by about ten speakers. For larger vocabularies or a larger number of speakers, this limit is considerably reduced.

One of the reasons why the systems fail to recognize speech spoken by a larger number of speakers is the considerable variation in the acoustic signals produced by different speakers. To begin with there are the differences in accent which often take the form of the substitution of one vowel or diphthong for another. It would be unreasonable to expect a machine to recognize that /bɑθ/ spoken with a Southern English accent was the same word as /bæθ/ spoken by a Northener, unless it had been specifically programmed. The number of variations, however, is not too large, and rules to account for most of them could probably be devised.

Another source of variation derives from the different physical sizes of the vocal tracts of different speakers. This causes the formants of children's voices to be about 30 per cent higher in frequency than those of men. Forgie and Forgie (1959) built a speech recognizer in which this source of variation was normalized by taking advantage of the correlation of vocal tract size and the pitch of the voice. The spectrum of the speech wave was formed with a 35-channel filter bank, and entered into a computer. The formant frequencies were determined, then normalized by means of the fundamental frequency. From these measurements the vowels in isolated words such as /b/-vowel-/t/ were recognized. It was reported that for twenty-one male and female speakers each producing ten vowels, and with no adjustment for speaker, the accuracy was 93 per cent.

Another method of normalization was introduced by Gerstman (1968). He normalized the vowels produced by a large number of speakers by means of the highest and lowest values of F1 and F2 of the vowels of each speaker. He then devised a vowel recognizer which misclassified only those vowels which were ambiguous to human listeners.

A further source of variability between speakers, and between different utterances of the same phrase spoken by the same speaker on different occasions, is the time course of the utterance. This varies to such an extent that it has been suggested that it should be ignored in speech recognition, and merely the sequence of acoustic events utilized. Others have suggested time normalization. The simplicity of the first course is attractive, but it ignores the fact that certain phonetic distinctions are made on the basis of the relative durations of events.

The latter course is probably more realistic, but it is difficult to employ until a better understanding has been obtained of the rules governing the rhythm of speech. In fast speech the durations of all phonemes are not uniformly reduced, so a straightforward time normalization algorithm may lead to error. The spectrum of the speech sound may also depend upon the speed of the utterance. Lindblom and Studdert-Kennedy (1967) showed that the vowel in a syllable such as /wɪw/ will be correctly perceived even though F1 and F2 never reach the values they would assume in the isolated vowel /ɪ/. Thus time normalization should take account of such factors as the rate at which formants are changing frequency.

Another factor which should be allowed for in a speech recognizer is co-articulation (Öhman, 1966a). The articulators move to the positions in which they will be required as soon as possible, so that the acoustic form of the current phoneme may be altered by the fact that some articulator, which is not involved in the production of this phoneme, is moving to the position in which it will be required for the production of the next phoneme.

Analogue feature recognition system

Despite these problems there is one speech recognizer, called the VIP-100, which is claimed by its builders to perform successfully enough for it to be used for practical tasks (Akroyd, 1974). A block diagram of its structure is shown in Fig. 10.4. The band-pass filters are sufficiently broad that a time resolution of 10 msec is attained. This is about the same as the DL of human listeners and may be necessary in order to follow some of the rapidly changing features of speech. The pre-processing circuits have a dynamic range of about 60 dB so that the energy in the loudest and quietest sounds can

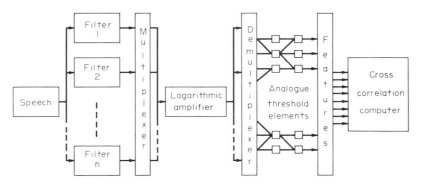

Fig. 10.4. Schematic diagram of the VIP-100 word recognizer.

be faithfully measured. This range is then reduced by logarithmic compression to about 20 dB. Differences in level between the channels then correspond to ratios in the original sound, so the system is fairly independent of overall loudness.

In many speech-recognition systems the formants were found as the positions of the peaks in the spectrum, and were easily missed. In this system, the regions of increasing or decreasing slope are detected instead. These can be found more reliably and are less dependent on the exact frequencies of the formants. The analogue threshold logic units (ATL) were designed to extract the features useful for recognition (Nelson *et al.*, 1967). Excitatory or inhibitory connections can be made, and the output represents the probability that a particular feature is present in the input. The actual connections were decided by the designers on the basis of their knowledge of speech, and a great deal of experimentation.

The outputs of the ATLs are connected to a small computer. Each word or phrase is stored in the computer as a sequence of extracted features. The current model has a vocabulary of thirty-two words or phrases. It is claimed that for a vocabulary of phonetically dissimilar words a recognition rate of 100 per cent is readily obtainable, but if the vocabulary contains similar words some errors may occur. The system must be adjusted for each individual speaker, but this can be done rapidly using the computer to store a number of examples of each member of the vocabulary.

Speaker-independent digit recognition

Another modern, small vocabulary recognition system has been reported by Sambur and Rabiner (1975). This digit-classification scheme segments the unknown word into three regions and then makes categorical judgements as to which of six broad acoustic classes each segment falls into. The classes are:

1. Voiced, noise-like consonant.
2. Unvoiced, noise-like consonant.
3. Vowel-like consonant.
4. Front vowel.
5. Middle vowel.
6. Back vowel.

The measurements made on the speech waveform include energy, zero-crossings, two-pole linear predictive coding analysis and normalized error of the linear predictive coding analysis. In order to make the system as speaker-independent as possible, many of these parameters are self-normalized. For example, in order to determine whether a segment is noise-like or nasal a statistical description is made for the zero-crossing rate of the entire utterance. One criterion for classifying a segment as noise-like is if its zero-crossing rate exceeds a level of one standard deviation above the mean during the segment. By using such relative measures a large degree of speaker independence has been achieved.

In a formal evaluation of the system employing twenty-five male and thirty female speakers, an error rate of 2.7 per cent was attained in a carefully controlled recording environment and a 5.6 per cent error rate for on-line recordings in a noisy computer room.

Continuous speech recognition

In the production of continuous speech (rather than isolated words) the variations mentioned above become more acute: pronunciation is less careful, speaker differences are underlined, speaking rate is less constant, co-articulation effects exist between words as well as within them. In addition new problems arise: the importance of a word in the message affects its stress and intonation and hence its acoustic realization. Although speech is perceived as a sequence of separate words, there is often little evidence of word boundaries. In attempting to recognize continuous speech, the machine is presented with an input message, which is imprecise, and in which not all of the information necessary for decoding is completely or unambiguously encoded. In such a situation a passive acoustic analyser plus pattern classifier is quite inadequate. Instead an active system which makes use of all the known constraints of language and which varies its analysis in the light of this knowledge is required.

There is ample evidence that human listeners make use of an extensive repertoire of linguistic cues and constraints in recognizing continuous speech. Klatt and Stevens (1973) tried to perform a phonetic transcription from some spectrograms of continuous speech. They succeeded in transcribing only 33 per cent of the phonemes completely correctly. For a further 40 per cent they achieved a correct partial transcription. When they used, in addition to the acoustic evidence, knowledge of the vocabulary, syntax and semantics of the utterance, they managed to identify 96 per cent of the words.

Pollack and Pickett (1964) have demonstrated that spoken fragments of sentences are not more than 90 per cent intelligible to human listeners if their syntactic and semantic structure is not apparent. A listener's application of linguistic knowledge often enables him to guess the remainder of a sentence after hearing the first few words. It appears that if machines are to approach human performance in the recognition of continuous speech, at least some linguistic expertise must be built into them.

Sources of linguistic knowledge

There are a number of sources of linguistic knowledge which may be built into a speech recognizer in order to improve its performance. These may be specified as acoustic, lexical, phonological, prosodic, syntactic, semantic and pragmatic.

The correlation between acoustic features and perceived phonetic sequences have been discussed in previous chapters. A mechanism must be provided for analysing the acoustic signal and extracting physical parameters which describe it. These parameters must then be segmented into phoneme-like units, and classified according to their structure. As this segmentation and classification cannot be expected to be completely reliable, probabalistic information reflecting the confidence of the decisions may be computed, or an "error set" containing the statistics of the misclassifications likely to be made may be included (Green and Ainsworth, 1972).

Lexical information is another source of linguistic knowledge. It is obviously useful to have a dictionary giving the phonetic composition of each word in the language. Dictionary entries may consist of ideal phonetic transcriptions, but it is useful to have multiple entries giving the variations in pronunciation unless these can be predicted by rules.

Phonological rules express the systematic ways in which the realization of words or phonemes may change with their environment. This knowledge helps to reconcile the results of acoustic–phonetic classification with the "ideal" word forms stored in the dictionary. Examples of phenomena for which context-dependent rules can be formulated are vowel reduction ("spectrogram" is usually pronounced/spektrəgrem/ not /spectrəʊgræm/) and deletion ("boundary" is /baʊndri/ not /baʊndəri/) and a number of consonant cluster corruptions ("did you" becomes /didʒu/ and "mostly" becomes /məʊsli/). A useful introduction to this work is given by Oshika *et al.* (1974).

The grammar of a language, expressed in a suitable form such as a set of syntactic rules, specifying how word sequences can be built up to form legal sentences is another source of useful knowledge.

Many cues to the syntactic structure of a sentence can be obtained from the prosodic features of the utterance. A knowledge of how duration, intensity, and fundamental frequency relate to stress, rhythm, intonation and juncture is required. These prosodic features can then be used to distinguish between such phrases as "they are (flying planes)" and "they (are flying) planes" or "light housekeeper" and "lighthouse keeper". They can also be used to indicate whether utterances like "this coat for five pounds" are to be interpreted as statements or questions. In addition, stress patterns can be used to indicate the parts of the utterance where the acoustic–phonetic information is most likely to be reliably extracted. Lea (1973) has investigated the extraction of prosodic features from energy and voicing parameters, and fundamental frequency contours.

If the world of discourse of the speech recognizer is sufficiently restricted it is sometimes possible to employ semantic information to choose between words or phrases which seem equally likely on phonetic, syntactic or other grounds.

Finally there is pragmatic information which allows the introduction of additional cues or constraints dependent upon the current context or situation. For instance, in an ongoing dialogue it may be possible to predict words or syntactic constructions which are likely to occur in the next utterance, or to impose additional semantic constraints.

In general, no one knowledge source can be relied upon to function perfectly, but suitably used in combination they should enable the speech recognizer to build a grammatical, meaningful and appropriate translation of the utterance. As any deduction made from information supplied by a source of knowledge may be shown by later processing to be in error, it is necessary to keep track of alternative possibilities in a suitable data structure.

A number of projects are being developed which attempt the problem of continuous speech recognition by combining the sources of linguistic knowledge in various ways.

Hierarchical systems

The most obvious approach to the design of a continuous speech-recognition system is to apply the sources of knowledge in series in a fixed order. Figure 10.5 shows a

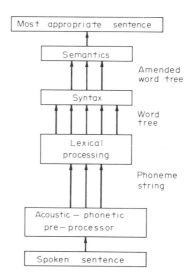

Fig. 10.5. The organization of an hierarchical speech-recognition system.

hypothetical system in which the acoustic processor attempts to translate the utterance into a string of phonemes. An "error set" and a dictionary are then used to compile a "word tree" summarizing all possible sequences of words which could have produced the phoneme string, together with probability measures for each pathway. The ungrammatical paths are then removed from the word tree by means of syntactic rules, and the probabilities of the remaining paths are modified accordingly. The semantic processor then decides which sentence is the most appropriate. One difficulty with this system is that it involves passing large quantities of data, sorted in complex data structures, between every stage. Green and Ainsworth (1973) implemented the first two stages of such a system and found that if the probability threshold for inclusion of a word in the tree was set low enough to ensure that the correct path was retained, the word trees (even for small vocabularies and short utterances) became unmanageably large.

A more elaborate hierarchical system has been developed by Tappert *et al.* (1973). The acoustic processor produces something akin to a broad phonetic transcription. The linguistic decoder, an error set and a phonetic lexicon are then employed to edit this transcription, divide it into words, and produce an orthographic output. Some phonological processing is incorporated in the acoustic processor, but prosodics, semantics and pragmatics are not currently used (Fig. 10.6).

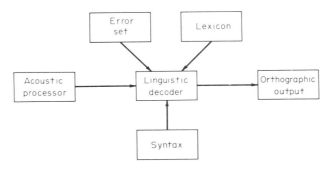

Fig. 10.6. System organization for the automatic recognition of continuous speech (ARCS).

Compared to an "ideal" phonetic form of the utterance, a machine transcription will contain errors of substitution, omission and insertion, introduced both by the speaker and by the machine. The probability that a given machine error has occurred in a given place can be deduced from the error set. The probability that a given string of phonemes corresponds to a given word can be estimated by matching each of its variants and choosing the best match. The score for a match will depend on the product of the probabilities of the machine errors necessary to transform the word into the string of phonemes in the machine transcription.

The next problem is to search a tree, defined by the syntax, of all possible utterances to find that path which requires the most likely set of error hypotheses. Since the tree is too large to be fully explored, the linguistic decoder must employ a heuristic search technique which finds a likely path in a reasonable time. Various searching techniques have been employed.

In experiments reported by Tappert (1974), one version of the system was evaluated on sentences taken from a 250-word vocabulary, with a finite-state grammar. A sentence-recognition accuracy of 54 per cent, corresponding to a word-recognition accuracy of 91 per cent, was achieved for a single speaker after training.

Hierarchical systems have been objected to on the grounds that they are inflexible. Each source of knowledge is utilized in a fixed sequence. A better approach might be to devise a system which calls for each source of knowledge when it is needed for the particular decision in hand.

Another objection is that, in the absence of feedback or feedforward paths, an error introduced at any stage will propagate through the system. In practice this means that at no stage can any possibility which is not definitely ruled out be ignored, no matter how unlikely it is. Consequently each stage must pass on to the next a great deal of data which must be processed, but most of which will ultimately be rejected. Thus although hierarchical systems may produce the right answer eventually, provided they contain all the appropriate sources of knowledge, they probably do not represent the most efficient way of achieving this goal.

Top-down systems

Top-down systems function according to the "hypothesize-and-test" paradigm. The "higher" levels of the system actively generate hypotheses which are tested by means of the acoustic data. A typical hypothesis might be that a certain word was spoken within a specified time range. A search would then be made for the sequence of acoustic features which that word might be expected to contain. This organization is similar to the "analysis-by-synthesis" idea of MacKay (1951) which has subsequently been invoked to explain many aspects of perception.

Top-down analysis may be thought of as growing a directed graph in which each node represents a partially decoded sentence. Each hypothesis defines a possible successor node, which is accepted or rejected on the results of the test. The process stops when a node representing a complete and acceptable sentence is found. The design problems include how to generate the hypotheses and assess their chances of success, how to back track up the graph when a hypothesis fails, and how to avoid re-entering a path which has failed before.

The voice-controlled data-management system of Barnett (1973) and Ritea (1974) is an example of the top-down philosophy. This is a speech-understanding system in which a spoken data-management language (150-word vocabulary, 35 syntactic rules) is used to access a data base containing information about submarine fleets. A typical utterance is "Print type where missiles greater than seven". A diagram of the system is shown in Fig. 10.7.

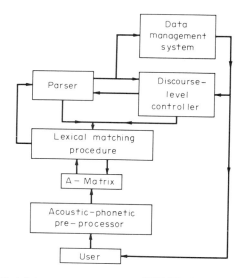

Fig. 10.7. Voice-controlled data management system (VDMS). An example of a "top-down" system.

The speech is sent to an "acoustic-phonetic processor" which forms an array of data called the "A-matrix". Each row of the A-matrix corresponds to a 10-msec speech segment. It contains a segment label (e.g. vowel-like, strong fricative), one or more phonemic labels with associated probability measures, and various acoustic parameter values.

A "Lexical Matching Procedure" verifies or rejects predicted words by matching against the A-matrix. The lexicon supplies an idealized phonemic form of the word which is expanded into a list of possible variants by phonological rules. Each variant is matched against the acoustic data on a syllable-by-syllable basis, using a further set of rules dealing with interactions over syllable boundaries. The parser uses "predictive linguistic constraints"—grammatical and semantic—to hypothesize phrases, and hence words, in the utterance. A non-directional method is used which can predict either to the left or right of already recognized phrases. The parser contains four major modules: a "classifier" which assigns a syntactic category to each word accepted by the lexical matching procedure; a "bottom driver" which predicts how discovered phrases might fit into complete sentences; a "top driver" which takes a predicted phrase and from it derives either a word to be matched or a shorter phrase to look for next; and a "side driver" which determines which part of an incomplete phrase (suggested by the bottom driver) the top driver should inspect next. Complete phrases which do not cover the entire utterance are returned to the input of the bottom driver, so that parsing can be driven recursively.

This "voice-controlled data management system" makes great use of pragmatic constraints. In the "discourse-level controller", a "user model" determines from the man-machine dialogue what "mode" the user is in (e.g. "interactive query", "report generation", "system log-in") and from this predicts additional grammatical constraints on the form of the next utterance. A "thematic memory" keeps track of the content words (nouns, verbs, etc.) which have occurred in the dialogue and predicts words which might occur in the next utterance on the assumption that recently mentioned concepts are likely to be used again. These predictions can be sent directly for lexical matching to initiate processing of an utterance. In the initial testing of this system, an average of 52 per cent of the sentences in realistic dialogues were correctly understood.

In the speech-understanding system of Walker (1974), top-down control is taken one stage further. The acoustic processor does not attempt any phonetic labelling other than a "phoneme-type" classification for each 10-msec interval. Instead there is a separate "word function" for each word in the vocabulary, and predictions are tested by calling these. A word function is a set of subroutines, written after detailed examination of the acoustic data for the word in a variety of contexts, which when called returns the probability of the word being present.

This system simulates a spoken dialogue with a "robot" about the assembly and repair of small mechanical devices, for example repairing a leaky tap. The task domain is simulated by a "world model" and analysis of an utterance (e.g. "what little brass parts are there in the box?") produces a program which operates on the world model. Analysis is controlled by a parser (Paxton, 1974). Every step on every path is assigned a "priority", path priorities are calculated from the products of step priorities, and the system follows the highest priority path. Four kinds of steps can be made: "syntactic" steps reflect the selection of a particular grammatical construction; "lexical" steps correspond to the choice of a particular word from a class; "word verification" steps (calls to "word function") follow each of the lexical steps, and "interparse-cooperation" steps avoid duplication of effort among competing paths. Step priorities for word-verification steps depend on the goodness of the word-function match and how well it aligns with adjacent words, while for syntactic and lexical steps the priorities depend on the syntactic and semantic cues and the world model information.

In processing seventy-one utterances, with forty-two word functions available, 62 per cent were correctly understood. The system is being developed so that other sources of knowledge can also be used in calculating the priorities.

The effectiveness of the top-down approach to artificial speech recognition depends on the predictive power of the higher levels of the system; that is on the capability of using syntactic, semantic and pragmatic information for making intelligent guesses. Thus top-down systems function best in problem domains where there are strong linguistic constraints on what the speaker is allowed to say. Prediction is perhaps most difficult in the initial stages when there are many possibilities. Prosodic information is potentially of great importance in restricting the hypothesis making. Lea *et al.* (1974) have proposed a "prosodically guided speech understanding strategy". In this scheme, a preliminary analysis, which relies heavily on the prosodic features of the utterance, yields both syntactic and lexical hypotheses which initialize the top-down processing, so that the parser needs to consider only a small set of possible structures at the outset. The likely syntactic structure of the sentence is derived from the phrase boundaries and the rhythm and stress patterns, while probable words are predicted from acoustic analysis and lexical matching of the stressed portions of the utterance. So far only the preliminary analysis modules of this system have been implemented.

Another speech-understanding system which is in the process of being developed is SPEECHLIS (Woods, 1974; Bates, 1974; Nash-Webber, 1974; Rovner *et al.*, 1974). The problem domain is again that of verbally assessing a data base. In this case the data base concerns the chemical analysis of the Apollo 11 moon rocks. A natural language interrogative computer system called LUNAR already exists which permits a wide range of sentence forms, such as:

"What is the average concentration of rubidium in high-alkali rocks?"
"List potassium rubidium ratios in samples not containing silicon."
"In what samples was titanium found?"

The full LUNAR system operates with a 3500-word lexicon, but SPEECHLIS currently uses a 250-word subset.

A feature of the development of SPEECHLIS is the use of "incremental simulation" (Woods *et al.*, 1974), whereby parts of the system not yet automated are replaced in simulations by humans in order to gain some feeling for how these parts might work. For instance, this technique enabled the authors to decide that there was no point in looking on a "bottom-up" scan for short function words ("a", "of", "the", etc.) which are usually unstressed, because of the high probability of accidental matches. It should be possible, however, to predict at a later stage from the syntax where the function words should occur, and from the semantics the most likely function words.

SPEECHLIS makes use of an initial word scan to pick out content words of three or more phonemes and words which are pragmatically likely to begin an utterance. The acoustic analyser, with the aid of phonological rules, assembles a "segment lattice" which represents probabalistically the alternative phonetic segmentations of the utterance, and the possible identities of each segment. Word matching is accomplished by a "lexical retrieval" program which finds words in the lexicon which could fit fragments of the segment lattice and a "word-verification" program which, given a particular word and a particular location, returns a matching score. Phonological rules and a "similarity matrix" (a kind of error set) are used in the matching algorithms.

The highly likely word matches found in the initial lexical scan, together with their scores, are entered in a "word lattice". The word-lattice data is used to initialize internal "theories", each of which represents a hypothesis that a certain collection of words are contained in the utterance, and includes syntactic and semantic structures linking these words, and associated scores. The "theories" grow and change as SPEECHLIS finds evidence for or against them. Eventually a "theory" representing a complete understanding of the utterance is evolved. Semantic knowledge is embodied in SPEECHLIS by means of a network representing the associations between words and concepts. This network is used to propose refinements to a "theory". For example, a word match for "chemical" suggests the concepts "chemical analysis" and "chemical elements". The semantic processor can formulate proposals to look for words like "analysis" and "element". If "analysis" is found, a new "theory" will be formed containing the two word matches and their semantic link.

As new "theories" are created by the semantic processor, each is examined to determine whether syntax might be used to develop it further by postulating grammatical structures linking the words in the "theory".

The "theory" building activities in SPEECHLIS are governed by a "control module" which creates "monitors". When a "monitor" is noticed, an "event" is created, pointing to the monitor and the new data. The basic control strategy is to form queues of proposals, theories and events, ordered by their likelihood scores, and to select elements from the top of these queues for processing.

Heterarchical systems

Instead of embodying the various sources of linguistic knowledge as a set of slaves controlled by a master, they can be organized to interact like a committee of experts. This is the structure of the HEARSAY speech-recognizing system developed by Reddy *et al.* (1973).

In HEARSAY, each source of linguistic knowledge is modelled as a self-contained "procedure" with three functions: the procedure decides when it has something useful to contribute, it makes contributions by originating hypotheses, and it tests the hypotheses made by the other procedures.

This system structure is inherently more flexible than the top-down structure, as the procedures which create the hypotheses and the ones which verify them depend on the current context rather than on any predetermined order. The HEARSAY framework also makes it easy to evaluate the contributions made by the various sources of knowledge (by disconnecting them); and to add new sources to the system.

Figure 10.8 shows the structure of the HEARSAY I system (Reddy *et al.*, 1973). It contains three independent recognizers which co-operate by individually suggesting and collectively verifying word hypotheses in order to fill gaps in a "currently accepted, partially recognized utterance". No hypothesis is adopted unless it is acceptable to all the recognizers. Recognition proceeds in alternate hypothesizing and verifying phases, controlled by a "recognition overlord". At the end of each hypothesizing phase, the "overlord" sends the hypothesis from the "most confident" recognizer to the others for verification.

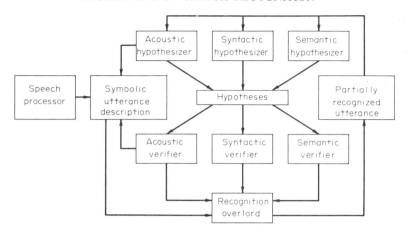

Fig. 10.8. Organization of a heterarchical, continuous speech recognition system.

It also stores the other hypotheses on a stack to enable back-tracking, and updates the partially recognized utterance after verification.

The preprocessor produces a "partial symbolic utterance description", including an estimate of the phonemic identity of each 10-msec segment, plus segmentation results and parameter values. This acoustic data, together with phonemic, phonological and lexical knowledge, is used by the "acoustic recognizer" to predict and verify syllables and words. Predictions are made by retrieving from the lexicon words which contain features which are present in the utterance description. Acoustic verification is similar to "word matching" described above.

The "syntactic recognizer" predicts words which occur immediately before or after the phrases present in the utterance description. Only local context is used in hypothesizing, but syntactic verification requires complete parsing of the partially recognized sentence.

Both semantic and pragmatic knowledge is embodied in the "semantic recognizer". The problem domain chosen was recognizing spoken chess moves (e.g. "knight to king's bishop three") in the context of a given board position. This is called "voice-chess". A chess program generates a list of possible moves at the current board position, together with an estimate of the likelihood of each move. In connection with the current "utterance description" and other semantic cues, this enables the production of likely words in the utterance to be made. In the voice-chess situation, the semantic recognizer has a powerful predictive capacity and usually generates the hypothesis, though the acoustic recognizer takes over in the presence of strong acoustic cues.

HEARSAY I was quite successful in the voice-chess domain. In one run, sixteen out of nineteen utterances were understood correctly. A new system, HEARSAY II, which also has a heterarchical structure is currently being developed by Lesser *et al.* (1974). This is to be implemented on a 16-processor mini-computer system, enabling the "sources of knowledge" to function in a self-activating, asynchronous, parallel manner. Co-operation is to be achieved through a global data base, or "blackboard" which allows the hypothesize-and-test paradigm to function on a variety of levels. The "blackboard" is a three-dimensional structure, the dimensions being level of representation (parametric, phonemic, lexical, etc.), time into the utterance, and alternative hypotheses for a given level and time. Hypotheses are represented by nodes in this structure, and interdependencies between hypotheses can be specified by links between the nodes.

CHAPTER 11

Models of Speech Perception

The preliminary processing of speech sounds is similar to the processing of all acoustic signals. The waves enter the ear where they are transformed from acoustic to mechanical vibrations by the eardrum and the ossicles. A travelling wave is set up in the cochlea, and a preliminary analysis based principally on frequency is performed. The signal is transformed into a set of neural discharges by the hair cells, and additional frequency selectivity is carried out. The resulting pattern of neural activity is transmitted to the auditory cortex by the tonotopic organization of the auditory system. Although the analysis to this stage is mostly in terms of frequency, the temporal pattern of the waves is retained as much as possible by synchronous discharges of the neurones.

Short-term auditory memory

Functionally at least, an auditory image consisting of the spectrum as a function of time is held in short-term memory whilst the first stage of processing, acoustic to phonemic, is carried out. Massaro (1974) has attempted to determine the size of this store. He presented sequential pairs of vowels to listeners, and asked them to identify the first vowel in the pair. The interval between the start of the first vowel and the start of the second was varied. He found that recognition performance improved up to 200–250 msec, suggesting that the short-term acoustic store is large enough to contain a syllable of speech.

An acoustic image is probably also required for the pitch of a sound to be established. There seems no reason to believe that the mechanism for determining the pitch of speech sounds is any different from that employed for other sounds (though the result may be used differently, especially in tone languages). The DL is about the same for speech and non-speech sounds, and the "pattern recognition" theory of pitch perception, involving the matching of harmonics in the dominant region of the spectrum, is particularly appropriate for dealing with speech-like sounds. This theory could explain why partially hearing persons with good low-frequency hearing, nevertheless speak with poor intonation.

Location of speech detector mechanisms

The strongest pathway from each ear is the contralateral one leading to the auditory cortex on the opposite side of the head. In the cortex there are many neurones which respond to features of sounds, and which are well suited to perform a classification of

120

speech sounds. Evidence has been obtained which indicates that if these neurones are fatigued by the repetition of certain sounds, misclassification of other related sounds results.

There is an accumulation of evidence which shows that for most people the right ear (and the left hemisphere of the brain) is better at recognizing speech than the left ear. Experiments in dichotic listening by normals and behavioural studies of patients with cortical lesions both support this view. The specialized speech detectors, however, are not located exclusively in the left hemisphere. It is possible to adapt the detectors in both sides of the brain in opposite directions simultaneously. Also in dichotic listening tasks, if the signal in one ear is masked by the addition of random noise, the performance of the other ear improves so that the total performance remains constant.

Motor theory of speech perception

Additional evidence for specialized speech detectors is provided by categorical perception. Speech discrimination is more acute across phoneme boundaries than within phonemes. It has been argued by Liberman *et al.* (1962) that this derives from the production of speech. Many experiments have supported the view that this enhanced discrimination is learned, and learned by long experience with a particular language. More precisely, it is possible that it is the connection between speech sounds and their associated articulatory gestures that is learned. If this is so, categorical perception simply reflects categorical production. With the human vocal apparatus it is not possible to produce sounds between /b/ and /d/ because one is generated with the lips and the other with the tongue. Consequently only /b/ and /d/ are heard in natural language, and so in artificial productions they are likewise classified by the perceptual mechanism.

Underlying this "motor theory" of speech perception is a more general theory of perception. Perception may be thought of as either an active or a passive process. In a passive process, features of the input pattern are detected, and combinations of these features excite second-order detectors, the triggering of which somehow gives rise to a "percept" (Fig. 11.1). In an active process, the parameters of a matching pattern are

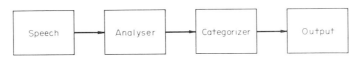

Fig. 11.1. A passive speech-recognition model.

adjusted by an "error signal" fed back from the comparator until a matching response is obtained (Fig. 11.2) (Mackay, 1967). In the motor theory of speech perception the parameters are the rules for speech production. Thus if a sound were perceived as speech, it would be perceived categorically.

It has been seen earlier that the acoustic manifestations of many phonemes are dependent on their context. This has led to the concept of "encodedness". The motor theory attempts to explain how such sounds are decoded. As each sound is received by the auditory system the "procedure" for producing it is determined, and compared with

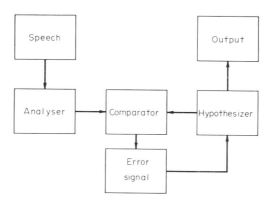

Fig. 11.2. An active speech-recognition model.

the repertoire of procedures. It can be argued that procedures are independent of context, so a simple "one-to-one" relationship can hold between perception and production, even though the relationship between each of these and the acoustics of speech is complex.

In order to test this hypothesis of a simple relationship, measurements have been made of the electromyographic signals involved in speech production. Despite encouraging results at first, a good deal of variability, both between contexts and speakers, has been found (Harris, 1971).

Auditory theory of speech perception

Fourcin (1975) has argued against the motor theory. One factor with which the motor theory does not explicitly deal is normalization. There are two ways in which this could be introduced into the theory. Either the input spectrum could be normalized, or the internal representation of the vocal tract to which the rules of production are applied could be normalized. In either case special problems are posed for the motor theory. In order for a baby to imitate his mother's speech, he must begin with knowledge of the scaling factors involved. This is not impossible, but it very much increases the complexity of the motor theory, which was initially introduced as a simple explanation of the complex relationship between perception and the acoustic structure of speech.

There are further considerations which suggest that audition, rather than production, is of primary importance in the acquisition of language. The motor theory would predict that because of inadequate feedback the deaf would have difficulty in speaking and the dumb would have difficulty in comprehending speech. It is true that the speech of the deaf is often less intelligible than that of persons with normal hearing, but cases have been found of persons unable to speak who have excellent comprehension (Fourcin and Lennenberg, 1973).

Another difference between the auditory and motor theories of speech perception is that in the former case the accuracy of speech discrimination will always be greater than the accuracy of speech production, and in the latter it will be the other way round.

Fourcin (1975) has performed preliminary experiments in which he has found that discrimination of intonation contours is as good by non-speakers as by persons with normal speech and hearing. Intonation by the deaf, on the other hand, is usually poor.

Even though "the motor theory" is perhaps not tenable, an active mechanism involving "analysis-by-synthesis" in the neural presentation of the auditory domain is certainly a possibility. This was first developed in detail as a model of speech perception by Halle and Stevens (Stevens, 1960; Halle and Stevens, 1962). In this scheme stored patterns of acoustic events are matched against incoming patterns and the mismatch signal guides the search through the repertoire of stored patterns. Categorical perception could be explained by such a scheme because the stored patterns would be derived from natural speech which lacks the intermediate patterns for consonants.

It is not clear at what level of abstraction the pattern matching should take place. It is possible that formant patterns might be involved, or higher level units such as linguistic features (Fant, 1967). It is possible that the analysis-by-synthesis scheme may be repeated at the phonological, lexical and semantic levels in a hierarchical structure (Fig. 11.3).

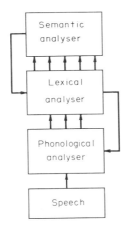

Fig. 11.3. A hierarchical model of speech recognition with feedback between the levels.

Models from automatic speech recognition

Models of speech perception have often gone hand in hand with schemes for automatic recognition. The hierarchical model, although not developed in any great detail, has been the generally accepted schema for some time. It has been realized that each level could be active or passive and that feedback or feedforward loops could exist between the levels, but the major flow of information is from the lower to the higher levels. In automatic speech recognition the hierarchical organization has generally been superseded because the acoustic data is so imprecise that some representation of every event must be preserved at each level in case it is of consequence. As a result of combinatorics, the amount of data becomes unmanageably large at the higher levels and the processing time unacceptable.

It is by no means certain that such objections apply in the case of the human speech-recognition mechanism. There are some 10 million billion neurones in the brain, and their organization is quite different from present-day digital computers.

The other organizations employed in automatic speech-recognition schemes, heterarchical and "top-down", may be more appropriate models. The "top-down" organization is the application of "analysis-by-synthesis" to the whole system, rather than at individual levels. It would be expected that other regions of the brain, triggered by other sensory modalities and internal cycles, would provide additional imputs to the "controller".

It is difficult to decide whether the "top-down" organization or the heterarchical organization is a more appropriate model of speech recognition. When the speech to be understood is corrupted by noise or spoken in an unfamiliar foreign language, the "top-down" model seems appropriate, but in the normal listening situation where the meaning is immediately grasped without conscious effort, the heterarchical model appeals. This impression, however, is purely subjective.

Conclusions

The gradual accumulation of experimental data, and the consequent refining of theory, is leading to a framework which is at least beginning to explain the complex phenomena of speech recognition. For example, consider the "cocktail-party" effect. If two spoken messages are mixed together, they are only understood after many repetitions. If the higher centres of the speech-recognition mechanism employ the "hypothesize-and-test" paradigm, the guesses can be refined on each repetition until the messages are ultimately understood. If the two messages are presented to separate ears, however, the neural pathways provide a mechanism whereby the messages can be kept separate, and the full information processing capacity concentrated on decoding one message at the expense of the other.

The methods which have been employed to unravel the mysteries of the speech-recognition mechanism are by no means exhausted. Techniques from experimental psychology, adaptation and masking, are only just beginning to be applied with speech-like stimuli. Advances are continually being made in neurophysiology which have implications for speech recognition. Developments in electronics and the availability of computers is helping to make the performing of complex experiments more feasible. Faster and larger computer systems are making it possible for more realistic automatic speech-recognition schemes to be tested. Finally, linguistics is being expanded so that the importance of the spoken word, as well as the written word, is being fully recognized.

References

Abel, S. M. (1972a) Duration discrimination of noise and tone bursts. *J. Acoust. Soc. Am.* **51**, 1219.

Abel, S. M. (1972b) Discrimination of temporal gaps. *J. Acoust. Soc. Am.* **52**, 519.

Abercrombie, D. (1965) *Studies in Phonetics and Linguistics*, Oxford University Press, London.

Ackroyd, M. H. (1974) Commercial applications of speech recognition. *IEE Digest No.* **1974/9**, 7.

Ades, A. E. (1974) Bilateral component in speech perception. *J. Acoust. Soc. Am.* **56**, 610.

Ainsworth, W. A. (1967a) Relative intelligibility of different transforms of clipped speech. *J. Acoust. Soc. Am.* **41**, 1272.

Ainsworth, W. A. (1967b) A speech synthesizer controlled by a PDP-8/338. *Third Decus European Seminar*, p. 1.

Ainsworth, W. A. (1968a) First formant transitions and the perception of synthetic semivowels. *J. Acoust. Soc. Am.* **44**, 689.

Ainsworth, W. A. (1968b) Perception of stop consonants in synthetic CV syllables. *Language and Speech* **11**, 139.

Ainsworth, W. A. (1972a) Duration as a cue in the recognition of synthetic vowels. *J. Acoust. Soc. Am.* **51**, 648.

Ainsworth, W. A. (1972b) A real-time speech synthesis system. *IEEE Trans. Electroacoust.* **AU-20**, 397.

Ainsworth, W. A. (1973) Durational cues in the perception of certain consonants. *Proc. Brit. Acoust. Soc.* **73**, SHA 5.

Ainsworth, W. A. (1974a) Influence of fundamental frequency on perceived vowel boundaries in English. *Speech Communication Seminar* **3**, 123. Almqvist & Wiksell, Stockholm.

Ainsworth, W. A. (1974b) Influence of precursive sequences on the perception of synthesized vowels. *Language and Speech* **17**, 103.

Ainsworth, W. A. (1974c) Performance of a speech synthesis system. *Int. J. Man-Machine Studies* **6**, 493.

Ainsworth, W. A. (1974d) Phoneme boundary shifts. *Eight Intn. Cong. Acoust.* **1**, 319, London.

Ainsworth, W. A. (1975a) Some effects of adaptation on phoneme boundaries. *Eighth Int. Cong. Phon. Sci.*, Leeds.

Ainsworth, W. A. (1975b) Intrinsic and extrinsic factors in vowel judgements. *Auditory Analysis and Speech Perception*, p. 103. Academic Press, London.

Ainsworth, W. A. and Millar, J. B. (1971) Methodology of experiments on the perception of synthesized vowels. *Language and Speech* **14**, 201.

Ainsworth, W. A. and Millar, J. B. (1972) The effect of relative formant amplitude on the perceived identity of synthetic vowels. *Language and Speech* **15**, 328.

Anthony, J. and Lawrence, W. (1962) A resonance analogue speech synthesizer. *Fourth Int. Cong. Acoust.*, paper G 43.

Askenfelt, A. (1973) Determination of difference limens at low frequencies. *STL-QPR* **2-3/1973**, 37.

Atal, B. S. and Schroeder, M. R. (1970) Adaptive predictive coding of speech signals. *Bell Syst. Tech. J.* **49**, 1973.

Atal, B. S. and Schroeder, M. R. (1974) Recent advances in predictive coding—applications to speech synthesis. *Speech Communication Seminar* **1**, 27. Almqvist & Wiksell, Stockholm.

Bailey, P. J. (1973) Perceptual adaptation for acoustic features in speech. *Speech Perception* **2**, 29.

Bailey, P. J. (1974) Perceptual adaptation for acoustical features in speech. *Speech Communication Seminar*, p. 47. Almqvist & Wiksell, Stockholm.

Barnett, J. (1973) A vocal data management system. *IEEE Audio Electroacoust.* **AU-21**, 185.

Bates, M. (1974) The use of syntax in a speech understanding system. *IEEE Symp. Speech Recognition*, p. 226.

Békésy, G. von (1928) Zur Theorie des Hörens; die Schwingungsform der Basilarmembran. *Physik. Zeits.* **29**, 793.

Békésy, G. von (1944) Uber die mechanische Frequenzanalyze in der Schnecke vershiedener Tiere. *Akust. Z.* **9**, 3.

Békésy, G. von (1960) *Experiments in Hearing*, McGraw-Hill, New York.

Bell, A. G. (1922) Prehistoric telephone days. *Nat. Geograph. Mag.* **41**, 223.

Bennett, D. C. (1968) Spectral form and duration cues in the recognition of English and German vowels. *Language and Speech* **11**, 65.

Berlin, C. I., Cullen, J. K., Lowe-Bell, S. S. and Berlin, H. L. (1974) Speech perception after hemispherectomy and temporal lobectomy. *Speech Communication Seminar*, p. 9. Almqvist & Wiksell, Stockholm.

Bezdel, W. and Chandler, H. J. (1965) Results of analysis and recognition of vowels by computer using zero-crossing data. *Proc. IEE* **112**, 2065.

Boer, E. de (1969) Reverse correlation. II. Initiation of nerve impulses in the inner ear. *Proc. Kon. Nederl. Akad. Wet. (Biol. Med.)* **72, 129**.

Bogdanski, D. F. and Galambos, R. (1960) Studies of the auditory system with implanted electrodes. *Neural Mechanisms of Auditory and Vestibular Systems*, p. 143. C. C. Thomas, Springfield, Ill.

Broadbent, D. E. and Gregory, M. (1964) Accuracy of recognition of speech presented to the right and left ears. *Q.J. Exptl Phychol.* **16**, 359.

Broadbent, D. E. and Ladefoged, P. (1960) Vowel judgements and adaptation level. *Proc. Royal Soc.* B, **151**, 384.

Brosnahan, L. F. and Malmberg, B. (1970) *Introduction to Phonetics*, Heffer, Cambridge.

Carlson, R., Fant, G. and Granström, B. (1974) Vowel perception and auditory theory. *Acustica* **31**, and *Auditory Analysis and Perception of Speech*, p. 55. Academic Press, London.

Carlson, R. and Granström, B. (1974) A phonetically oriented programming language for rule description of speech. *Speech Communication Seminar* **2**, 247. Almqvist & Wiksell, Stockholm.

Carterette, E. C. (1956) Loudness adaptation for bands of noise. *J. Acoust. Soc. Am.* **28**, 865.

Carterrete, E. C. and Jones, M. H. (1974) *Informal Speech: Phonemic and Alphabetic Texts with Statistical Analyses*, University of California Press, Berkeley and Los Angeles.

Causse, R. and Chavasse, P. (1947) Études sur la fatigue auditive. *Année Psychol.* **43–44**, 265.

Cherry, E. C. (1953) Some experiments on the recognition of speech, with one and two ears. *J. Acoust. Soc. Am.* **25**, 975.

Chomsky, N. and Halle, M. (1968) *The Sound Pattern of English*, Harper & Row, New York.

Churcher, B. G. (1935) A loudness scale for industrial noise measurements. *J. Acoust. Soc. Am.* **6**, 216.

Classe, A. (1939) *The Rhythm of English Prose*, Blackwell, Oxford.

Cohen, A., Slis, I. H. and 't Hart, J. (1967) On tolerance and intolerance in vowel perception. *Phonetica* **16**, 65.

Coker, C. H. (1968) Speech synthesis with a parametric articulatory model. *Proc. Speech Symp.* Kyoto, Japan.

Cooley, J. W. and Tukey, J. W. (1965) An algorithm for the machine calculation of complex Fourier series. *Math. of Comput.* **19**, 297.

Cooper, F. S., Liberman, A. M. and Borst, J. M. (1951) The inter-conversion of audible and visible patterns as a basis for research in the perception of speech. *Proc. Nat. Acad. Sci.* **37**, 318.

Cooper, W. E. (1974) Adaptation of phonetic feature analyzers for place of articulation. *J. Acoust. Soc. Am.* **56**, 617.

Creelman, C. D. (1962) Human discrimination of auditory duration. *J. Acoust. Soc. Am.* **34**, 582.

Cullen, J. K., Thomson, C. L., Hughes, L. F. and Berlin, C. I. (1974) Information additivity in dichotic stop-vowel perception tasks. *Speech Communication Seminar* **3**, 31. Alqvist & Wiksell, Stockholm.

Cutting, J. E. (1972) Ear advantage for stops and liquids in initial and final position. *Haskins Lab. Status Report of Speech Research* SR-31/32, 57.

Darwin, C. J. (1971) Ear differences in the recall of fricatives and vowels. *Q.J. Exptl Psychol.* **23**, 46.

Davis, H. (1958) A mechano- electrical theory of cochlear action. *Ann. Otol. Rhinol. Laryngol.* **67**, 789.

Davis, K. H., Biddulph, R. and Balashek, S. (1952) Automatic recognition of spoken digits. *J. Acoust. Soc. Am.* **24**, 637.

Debiasi, G. B., Depoli, G., Mian, G. A., Mildonian, G. and Offelli, C. (1974) Italian speech synthesis from unrestricted text for an automatic answerback system. *Eight Int. Cong. Acoust.* **1**, 296, London.

Delattre, P. C., Liberman, A. M., Cooper, F. S. and Gerstman, L. J. (1952) An experimental study of the acoustic determinants of vowel color. *Word* **8**, 195.

Denes, P. B. (1963) On the statistics of spoken English. *J. Acoust. Soc. Am.* **35**, 892.

Dennis, J. B. (1962) Computer control of an analog vocal tract. *Speech Communication Seminar*, Stockholm.

Dudley, H. (1939) The vocoder. *Bell Labs. Record.* **17**, 122.

Dudley, H. and Balashek, S. (1958) Automatic recognition of phonetic patterns in speech. *J. Acoust. Soc. Am.* **30**, 721.

Dudley, H. and Tarnoczy, T. H. (1950) The speaking machine of Wolfgang von Kempelen. *J. Acoust. Soc. Am.* **22**, 740.

Dunn, H. K. (1950) The calculation of vowel resonances, and an electrical vocal tract. *J. Acoust. Soc. Am.* **22**, 740.

Egan, J. P. (1948) Articulation testing methods. *Laryngoscope* **58**, 955.

Eimas, P. D., Cooper, W. E. and Corbit, J. D. (1973) Some properties of linguistic feature detectors. *Perception and Psychophysics* **13**, 247.

Eimas, P. D. and Corbit, J. D. (1973) Selective adaptation of linguistic feature detectors. *Cognitive Psychol.* **4**, 99.

Evans, E. F. (1968) Cortical representation. *Hearing Mechanisms in Vertebrates*, p. 272. Churchill, London.

Evans, E. F. (1970) Narrow "tuning" of cochlear nerve fibre responses in the guinea pig. *J. Physiol.* **206**, 14.

Evans, E. F. (1971) Central mechanisms relevant to the neural analysis of simple and complex sounds. *Pattern Recognition in Biological and Technical Systems*, Springer, Heidelberg.

Evans, E. F. (1972) The frequency response and other properties of single fibres in the guinea pig cochlear nerve. *J. Physiol.* **226**, 263.

Evans, E. F. (1974) The sharpening of cochlear frequency selectivity in the normal and abnormal cochlear. *Int. Cong. Audiology*, Paris.

Evans, E. F. and Nelson, P. G. (1973) On the functional relationship between the dorsal and ventral cochlear nucleus of the cat. *Exptl Brain Res.* **17**, 428.

Evans, E. F., Rosenberg, J. and Wilson, J. P. (1970) The effective bandwidth of cochlear nerve fibres. *J. Physiol.* **207**, 62.

Evans, E. F., Rosenberg, J. and Wilson, J. P. (1971) The frequency resolving power of the cochlea. *J. Physiol.* **216**, 58.

Evans, E. F. and Whitfield, I. C. (1964) Classification of unit responses in the auditory cortex of the unanaesthetised and unrestrained cat. *J. Physiol.* **171**, 476.

Evans, E. F. and Wilson, J. P. (1973) Frequency selectivity of the cochlea. *Basic Mechanisms of Hearing*, Academic Press, New York.

Fabre, P. (1959) La glottographie électriques en haute fréquence, particularitiés de l'appareillage. *Comptes Rendus des Sciences de la Socitete de Biologie et de ses Filiales* **153**, 1361.

Fairbanks, G., Everitt, W. L. and Jaeger, R. P. (1954) Method for time or frequency compression of speech. *IRE Trans. on Audio*, **AU-2**, 7.

Fant, G. (1956) On the predictability of formant levels and spectrum envelopes from formant frequencies. *For Roman Jakobson*, Mouton, s'Gravenhage.

Fant, G. (1960) *Acoustic Theory of Speech Production*, Mouton, s'Gravenhage.

Fant, G. (1967) Auditory patterns of speech, *Models for the Perception of Speech and Visual Form*, p. 111. M.I.T. Press, Cambridge, Mass.

Fant, G. and Mártony, J. (1962) Instrumentation for parametric synthesis (OVE II). *Speech Transmission Lab. Q.P.R.*, p. 18. Stockholm.

Flanagan, J. L. (1955) A difference limen for vowel formant frequency. *J. Acoust. Soc. Am.* **27**, 613.

Flanagan, J. L. (1957) Difference limen for formant amplitude. *J. Speech Hearing Disorders* **22**, 205.

Flanagan, J. L. (1965) *Speech Analysis, Synthesis and Perception*, Springer, Berlin.

Flanagan, J. L. (1972) Voices of men and machines, *J. Acoust. Soc. Am.* **51**, 1375.

Flanagan, J. L., Coker, C. H., Rabiner, L. R., Schafer, R. W. and Umeda, N. (1970) Synthetic voices for computers. *IEEE Spectrum* **7**, 22.

Flanagan, J. L. and Saslow, M. G. (1958) Pitch discrimination for synthetic vowels. *J. Acoust. Soc. Am.* **10**, 435.

Fletcher, H. (1929) *Speech and Hearing*, Van Nostrand, New York.

Fletcher, H. (1938) Loudness, masking and their relation to the hearing process and the problem of noise measurement. *J. Acoust. Soc. Am.* **9**, 275.

Fletcher, H. and Munson, W. A. (1937) Relation between loudness and masking. *J. Acoust. Soc. Am.* **9**, 1.

Forgie, J. W. and Forgie, C. D. (1959) Results obtained from a vowel recognition computer program. *J. Acoust. Soc. Am.* **31**, 1480.

Fourcin, A. (1960) A potential dividing function generator for the control of speech synthesis. *J. Acoust. Soc. Am.* **32**, 1501.

Fourcin, A. J. (1968) Speech source inference. *IEEE Trans. Audio Electroacoust.* **AU-16**, 65.

Fourcin, A. J. (1975) Speech perception in the absence of speech productive ability. *Language and Cognitive Deficits and Retardation*, Butterworth, London.

Fourcin, A. J. and Abberton, E. (1971) First applications of a new laryngograph. *Medical and Biological Illustration* **21**, **172**.

Fourcin, A. J. and Lenneberg, E. (1973) Language development in the absence of expressive speech. *Foundations of Language Development*, IBRO–UNESCO.

French, N. R., Carter, C. W. and Koenig, W. (1930). The words and sounds of telephone conversations. *Bell. System Tech. J.* **9**, 290.

French, N. R. and Steinberg, J. C. (1947) Factors governing the intelligibility of speech sounds. *J. Acoust. Soc. Am.* **19**, 90.

Fry, D. B. (1955) Duration and intensity as physical correlates of linguistic stress. *J. Acoust. Soc. Am.* **27**, 765.

Fry, D. B. (1958) Experiments in the perception of stress. *Language and Speech* **1**, 126.

Fry, D. B., Abramson, A. S., Eimas, P. D. and Liberman, A. M. (1962) The identification and discrimination of synthetic vowels. *Language and Speech* **5**, 171.

Fry, D. B. and Denes, P. (1958) The solution of some fundamental problems in mechanical speech recognition. *Language and Speech* **1**, 35.

Fujimura, O. (1962) Analysis of nasal consonants. *J. Acoust. Soc. Am.* **34**, 1865.

Fujisaki, H. and Kawashima, T. (1968) The roles of pitch and higher formants in the perception of vowels. *IEEE Trans. Audio Electroacoust.* **AU-16**, 73.

Fujisaki, H., Nakamura, K. and Imoto, T. (1975) Auditory perception of duration of speech and non-speech stimuli. *Auditory Analysis and Perception of Speech*, p. 197. Academic Press, London.

Fujisaki, H. and Kawashima, T. (1971) A model for speech perception—quantitative analysis of categorical effects in discrimination. *Annual Report of the Engineering Research Institute, University of Tokyo*, **30**, 59.

Gabor, D. (1946) Theory of communication. *J. Inst. Elect. Engrs* **93**, 429.

Garner, W. R. and Miller, G. A. (1944) Differential sensitivity to intensity as a function of the duration of the comparison tone. *J. Exptl Psychol.* **34**, 450.

Gerstman, L. J. (1968) Classification of self-normalized vowels. *IEEE Trans. Audio Electroacoust.* **AU-16**, 78.

Gimson, A. C. (1970) *An Introduction to the Pronunciation of English*, Arnold, London.

Green, P. D. (1971) *Temporal Characteristics of Spoken Consonants as Discriminants in Automatic Speech Recognition*, Ph.D. Thesis, University of Keele.

Green, P. D. and Ainsworth, W. A. (1972) Towards the automatic recognition of spoken Basic English. *Machine Perception of Patterns and Pictures*, Inst. of Physics Conf. Series No. 13, p. 161.

Green, P. D. and Ainsworth, W. A. (1973) Development of a system for the automatic recognition of spoken Basic English. *Brit. Acoust. Soc.* 1973 Spring Meeting.

Haggard, M. P. (1971) Encoding and the REA for speech signals. *Q.J. Exptl Psychol.* **23**, 34.

Haggard, M. P., Ambler, S. and Callow, M. (1970) Pitch as a voicing cue. *J. Acoust. Soc. Am.* **47**, 613.

Halle, M., Hughes, G. W. and Radley, J.-P. A. (1957) Acoustic properties of stop consonants. *J. Acoust. Soc. Am.* **29**, 107.

Halle, M. and Stevens, K. N. (1962) Speech recognition: a model and a programme for research. *IRE Trans.* **PGIT IT-8**, 155.

Halliday, M. A. K. (1963) The tones of English. *Archivum Linguisticum* **15**, 1.

Harris, K. S. (1958) Cues for the discrimination of American English fricatives in spoken syllables. *Language and Speech* **1**, 1.

Harris, K. S. (1971) Vowel stress and articulatory reorganization. *Haskins Laboratories Status Report on Speech Research* **SR-28**, 167.

Harris, K. S., Hoffman, H. S., Liberman, A. M., Delattre, P. C. and Cooper, F. S. (1958) Effects of third-formant transitions on the perception of voiced stop consonants. *J. Acoust. Soc. Am.* **30**, 1035.

Hecker, M. H. L. (1962) Studies of nasal consonants with an articulatory speech synthesizer. *J. Acoust. Soc. Am.* **34**, 179.

Heinz, J. M. and Stevens, K. N. (1961) On the properties of voiceless fricative consonants. *J. Acoust. Soc. Am.* **33**, 589.

Hoffman, H. S. (1958) Study of some cues in the perception of voiced stop consonants. *J. Acoust. Soc. Am.* **30**, 1035.

Hollbrook, A. and Fairbanks, G. (1962) Diphthong formants and their movements. *J. Speech Hear Res.* **5**, 38.

Holmes, J. N. (1972) *Speech Synthesis*, Mills & Boon, London.

Holmes, J. N. (1973) The influence of the glottal waveform on the naturalness of speech from a parallel-formant synthesizer. *IEEE Trans. Audio Electroacoust.* **AU-21**, 298.

Holmes, J. N., Mattingly, I. G. and Shearme, J. N. (1964) Speech synthesis by rule. *Language and Speech* **7**, 127.

Houtgast, T. (1972) Psychophysical evidence for lateral inhibition in hearing, *J. Acoust. Soc. Am.* **51**, 1885.

Houtgast, T. (1973) Psychophysical experiments on "tuning curves" and "two-tone inhibition". *Acustica* **29**, 168.

Hubel, D. H. (1957) Tungsten microelectrodes for recording from single units. *Science* **125**, 549.

Hubel, D. H. and Wiesel, T. N. (1962) Receptive fields, binocular interaction and functional architecture in the cat's visual cortex. *J. Physiol.* **160**, 106.

Huggins, A. W. F. (1975) On isochrony and syntax. *Auditory Analysis and Perception of Speech*, p. 455. Academic Press, London.

Hughes, G. W. and Halle, M. (1956) Spectral properties of fricative consonants. *J. Acoust. Soc. Am.* **28**, 303.

Hyde, S. R. (1969) Perception of very brief sounds. *Second Int. Congr. Appl. Linguistics*, Cambridge.

Jassem, W. (1975) Normalization of F0 curves. *Auditory Analysis and Perception of Speech*, p. 523. Academic Press, London.

Jakobson, R., Fant, C. G. M. and Halle, M. (1952) *Preliminaries to Speech Analysis*, Tech. Rep. No. 13, M.I.T., Cambridge, Mass.

Johnstone, B. M. and Boyle, A. J. F. (1967) Basilar membrane vibration examined with the Mössbauer technique. *Science* **158**, 389.

Johnstone, B. M., Taylor, K. J. and Boyle, A. J. (1970) Mechanics of the guinea pig cochlea. *J. Acoust. Soc. Am.* **47**, 504.

Jones, D. (1949) *Outline of English Phonetics*, Heffer, Cambridge.

Jordan, B. P. and Kelly, L. C. (1974) A comparison of the speech quality of a linear predictive coder and a channel vocoder. *Eighth Int. Cong. Acoust.* **1**, 283. London.

Katsuki, Y., Suga, N. and Kanno, Y. (1962) Neural mechanisms of the peripheral and central auditory systems in monkeys. *J. Acoust. Soc. Am.* **34**, 1396.

Katsuki, Y., Watenabe, T. and Maruyama, N. (1959) Activity of and neurones in upper levels of brain of cat. *J. Neurophysiol.* **22**, 343.

Kelly, J. L. and Gerstman, J. L. (1961) An artificial talker driven from a phonetic input. *J. Acoust. Soc. Am.* **33**, 835.

Kersta, L. G. (1948) Amplitude cross-section representation with the sound spectrograph. *J. Acoust. Soc. Am.* **20**, 796.

Kiang, N. Y-S., Watenabe, T., Thomas, E. C. and Clark, L. F. (1965) *Discharge Patterns of Single Fibres in the Cat's Auditory Nerve*, M.I.T. Press, Cambridge, Mass.

Kimura, D. (1961) Some effects of temporal lobe damage on auditory perception. *Can. J. Psychol.* **15**, 166.

Kimura, D. (1964) Left-right differences in the perception of melodies. *Q.J. Exptl Psychol.* **14**, 355.

Kirstein, E. F. (1973) The lag effect in dichotic speech perception. *Haskins Laboratories: Status Report on Speech Research*, SR-35/36.

Klatt, D. H. and Stevens, K. N. (1973) On the automatic recognition of continuous speech: implications from a spectrogram-reading experiment. *IEEE Trans. Audio Electroacoust.* **AU-21**, 210.

Klumpp, R. G. and Webster, J. C. (1961) Intelligibility of time compressed speech. *J. Acoust. Soc. Am.* **33**, 265.

Koch, R. F. (1972) The Ambichron: an electronic time compressor for audio. *Conference on Speech Communication and Processing*, IEEE Cat. No. 72 CHO 596-7 AE, p. 45.

Koenig, W., Dunn, H. K. and Lacy, L. Y. (1946) The sound spectrograph. *J. Acoust. Soc. Am.* **17**, 19.

Kozhevnikov, N. A. and Chistovich, L. A. (1965) Speech: articulation and perception. *JPRS/30543*, Washington D.C.

Laver, J. D. M. H. (1965) Variability in vowel perception. *Language and Speech* **8**, 95.

Lavington, S. H. (1968) *Measurement System for Automatic Speech Recognition*, Ph.D. Thesis, University of Manchester.

Lawrence, W. (1953) The synthesis of speech from signals which have a low information rate. *Communication Theory*, p. 460. Butterworth, London.

Lea, W. A. (1973) An approach to syntactic recognition without phonemics. *IEEE Trans. Audio Electroacoust.* **AU-21**, 249.

Lea, W. A., Medress, M. F. and Skinner, T. E. (1974) A prosodically-guided speech understanding strategy, *IEEE Symp. on Speech Recognition*, p. 38.

Lenneberg, E. H. (1967) *Biological Foundations of Language*, John Wiley, New York.

Lesser, V. R., Fennell, R. D., Erman, L. D. and Reddy, D. R. (1974) Organization of the HEARSAY II speech understanding system, *IEEE Symp. on Speech Recognition*, p. 11.

Lettvin, J. Y., Maturana, H. R., McCulloch, W. S. and Pitts, W. H. (1959) What the frog's eye tells the frog's brain. *Proc. I.R.E.* **47**, 1940.

Liberman, A. M., Cooper, F. S., Harris, K. S. and MacNeilage, P. F. (1962) A motor theory of speech perception. *Speech Communication Seminar*, Stockholm.

Liberman, A. M., Cooper, F. S., Shankweiler, D. P. and Studdert-Kennedy, M. (1967) Perception of the speech code. *Psych. Rev.* **74**, 431.

Liberman, A. M., Delattre, P. C. and Cooper, F. S. (1958) Some cues for the distinction between voiced and voiceless stops in initial position. *Language and Speech*, **1**, 153.

Liberman, A. M., Delattre, P. C., Cooper, F. S. and Gerstman, L. J. (1954) The role of consonant–vowel transitions in the perception of the stop and nasal consonants. *Psych. Monographs* **68**, 1.

Liberman, A. M., Delattre, P. C., Gerstman, L. J. and Cooper, F. S. (1956) Tempo of frequency change as a cue for distinguishing classes of speech sounds. *J. Exptl Psychol.* **52**, 127.

Liberman, A. M., Harris, K. S., Hoffman, H. S. and Griffith, B. C. (1957) The discrimination of speech sounds within and across phoneme boundaries. *J. Exptl Psychol.* **54**, 358.

Liberman, A. M., Ingeman, F., Lisker, L., Delattre, P. and Cooper, F. S. (1959) Minimal rules for synthesizing speech. *J. Acoust. Soc. Am.* **31**, 1490.

Licklider, J. C. R. (1946) Effects of amplitude distortion upon the intelligibility of speech. *J. Acoust. Soc. Am.* **18**, 429.

Licklider, J. C. R. and Miller, G. A. (1951) The perception of speech. *Handbook of Experimental Psychology*, p. 1040. Wiley, New York.

Licklider, J. C. R. and Pollack, I. (1948) Effects of differentiation, integration, and infinite peak clipping upon the intelligibility of speech. *J. Acoust. Soc. Am.* **20**, 42.

Lifshitz, S. (1933) Two integral laws of sound perception relating loudness and apparent duration of sound impulses, *J. Acoust. Soc. Am.* **5**, 31.

Liljencrants, J. C. W. A. (1968) The OVE III speech synthesizer. *IEEE Trans. Audio Electroacoust.* **AU-16**, 137.

Lindblom, B. (1963) Spectrographic study of vowel reduction. *J. Acoust. Soc. Am.* **35**, 1773.

Lindblom, B. E. F. (1975) Some temporal regularities in spoken Swedish. *Auditory Analysis and Perception of Speech*, p. 387. Academic Press, London.

Lindblom, B. and Studdert-Kennedy, M. (1967) On the role of formant transitions in vowel recognition. *J. Acoust. Soc. Am.* **42**, 830.

Lisker, L. (1957a) Closure duration and the intervocalic voiced–voiceless distinction in English. *Language* **33**, 41.

Lisker, L. (1957b) Minimal cues for separating /w,r,l,y/ in intervocalic position. *Word* **13**, 256.

Lisker, L. and Abramson, A. S. (1967) Some effects of context on voice onset time in English stops. *Language and Speech* **10**, 1.

MacKay, D. M. (1951) Mindlike behaviour in artefacts. *Brit. J. Phil. Sci.* **2**, 105.

MacKay, D. M. (1967) Ways of looking at perception. *Models for the Perception of Speech and Visual Form*, p. 25. M.I.T. Press, Cambridge, Mass.

McLarnon, E. and Holmes, J. N. (1974) Experiments with a variable-frame-rate coding scheme applied to formant synthesizer control signals. *Eighth Int. Cong. Acoust.* **1**, 281, London.

Massaro, D. W. (1974) Perceptual units in speech recognition. *J. Exptl Psychol.* **102**, 199.

Mattingly, I. G. (1971) Synthesis by rule as a tool for phonological research. *Language and Speech* **14**, 47.

Meeker, W. F. and Nelson, A. L. (1964) Vocoder evaluation research. *Air Force Cambridge Res. Lab. Report AFCRL-64-46*, 1.

Millar, J. B. and Ainsworth, W. A. (1972) Identification of synthetic isolated vowels and vowels in h–d context. *Acustica* **27**, 278.

Miller, G. A., Heise, G. A. and Lichten, W. (1951) The intelligibility of speech as a function of the context of the test materials. *J. Exptl Psychol.* **41**, 329.

Miller, G. A. and Licklider, J. C. R. (1950) The intelligibility of interrupted speech. *J. Acoust. Soc. Am.* **22**, 167.

Miller, G. and Nicely, P. (1955) An analysis of perceptual confusions among some English consonants. *J. Acoust. Soc. Am.* **27**, 338.

Miller, R. L. (1953) Auditory tests with synthetic vowels. *J. Acoust. Soc. Am.* **25**, 1533.

Miyawaki, K., Liberman, A. M., Fujimura, O., Strange, W. and Jenkins, J. J. (1975) Cross-language study of the perception of the F3 cue for /r/ versus /l/ in speech- and non-speech-like patterns. *Auditory Analysis and Perception of Speech*, p. 339. Academic Press, London.

Morse, P. M. (1948) *Vibration and Sound*, McGraw-Hill, New York.

Munson, W. A. (1947) The growth of auditory sensation. *J. Acoust. Soc. Am.* **19**, 584.

Nakata, K. (1959) Synthesis of nasal consonants by a terminal-analog synthesizer. *J. Radio Res. Lab. (Tokyo)* **6**, 243.

Nash-Webber, B. (1974) Semantic support for a speech understanding system. *IEEE Symposium Speech Recognition*, p. 244.

Nelson, A. L. Herscher, M. B., Martin, T. B., Zadell, H. J. and Falter, J. W. (1967) Acoustic recognition by analog feature-abstraction techniques. *Models for the Perception of Speech and Visual Form*, p. 428. M.I.T. Press.

Nelson, P. G., Erulkar S. D. and Bryan J. S. (1966) Responses of units of the inferior colliculus to time-varying acoustic stimuli. *J. Neurophysiol.* **29**, 834.

Newell, A. *et al.* (1971) *Speech Understanding Systems*, Carnegie-Mellon University, Pittsburgh.

Nordmark, J. O. (1968) Mechanisms of frequency discrimination. *J. Acoust. Soc. Am.* **44**, 1533.

O'Connor, J. D. (1973) *Phonetics*, Penguin Books, London.

O'Connor, J. D., Gerstman, L. J., Liberman, A. M., Delattre, P. C. and Cooper, F. S. (1957) Acoustic cues for the perception of initial /w,j,r,l/ in English. *Word* **13**, 24.

Ohala, J. J. (1975) The temporal regulation of speech. *Auditory Analysis and Perception of Speech*, p. 431. Academic Press, London.

Öhman, S. E. G. (1966a) Co-articulation in VCV utterances: spectrographic measurements. *J. Acoust. Soc. Am.* **39**, 151.

Öhman, S. E. G. (1966b) Perception of segments of VCCV utterances. *J. Acoust. Soc.* **40**, 979.

Oshika, B. T., Zue, V. W., Weeks, R. V., Neu, H. and Aurback, J. (1974) The role of phonological rules in speech understanding research. *IEEE Symp. on Speech Recognition*, p. 204.

Paget, R. (1930) *Human Speech; Some Observations, Experiments, and Conclusions as to its Nature, Origin, Purpose and Possible Improvement of Human Speech*, Harcourt, New York.

Paxton, W. H. (1974) A best-first parser. *IEEE Symp. Speech Recognition*, p. 218.

Peterson, G. E. and Barney, H. L. (1952) Control methods used in a study of the vowels. *J. Acoust. Soc. Am.* **24**, 175.

Peterson, G. E. and Lehiste, I. (1960) Duration of syllable nuclei in English. *J. Acoust. Soc. Am.* **32**, 693.

Pike, K. L. (1945) *The Intonation of American English*, University of Michigan Press, Michigan.

Pisoni, D. B. (1973) Auditory and phonetic memory codes in the discrimination of consonants and vowels. *Perception and Psychophysics* **13**, 253.

Pollack, I. and Pickett, J. M. (1964) The intelligibility of excerpts from conversation. *Language and Speech* **6**, 165.

Pols, L. C. W., van der Kamp, L. J. and Plomp, R. (1969) Perceptual and physical space of vowel sounds. *J. Acoust. Soc. Am.* **46**, 458.

Porter, R. J. (1972) An investigation of the effects of delayed channel on the perception of dichotically presented speech and nonspeech sounds. *Dissert. Abstr.* **33**, 2841-2-13.

Porter, R. J. (1974) The dichotic lag effect: implications for the central processing of speech. *Speech Communication Seminar*, 3, 21. Almqvist & Wiksell, Stockholm.

Potter, R. K., Kopp, G. A. and Green, H. C. (1947) *Visible Speech*, van Nostrand, New York.

Purton, R. F. (1968) Speech recognition using auto-correlation analysis. *IEEE Trans. Audio Electroacoust.* **AU-16**, 2235.

Rabiner, L. R., Jackson, L. B., Schafer, R. W. and Coker, C. H. (1971) Digital hardware for speech synthesis. *Seventh Int. Cong. Acoust.*, Budapest.

Rawnsley, A. I. and Harris, J. D. (1952) Studies in short duration fatigue: II. Recovery time. *J. Exptl Psychol.* **43**, 138.

Reddy, D. R. (1967) Computer recognition of connected speech. *J. Acoust. Soc. Am.* **42**, 329.

Reddy, D. R., Erman, L. D. and Neely, R. B. (1973) A model and a system for machine recognition of speech. *IEEE Trans. Audio Electroacoust* **AU-21**, 229.

Rhode, W. S. (1971) Observation of the vibrations of the basilar membrane in squirrel monkeys using the Mössbauer technique. *J. Acoust. Soc. Am.* **49**, 1218.

Riesz, R. R. (1928) Differential intensity sensitivity of the ear for pure tones. *Phys. Rev.* **31**, 867.

Ritea, H. B. (1974) A voice-controlled data management system. *IEEE Symp. on Speech Recognition*, p. 28.

Rose, J. E., Brugge, J. F., Anderson, D. J. and Hind, J. E. (1968) Pattern of activity in single auditory nerve fibres of the squirrel monkey. *Hearing Mechanisms in Vertebrates*, p. 144. Churchill, London.

Rose, J. E., Greenwood, D. D., Goldberg, J. M. and Hind, J. E. (1963) Some discharge characteristics of single neurones in inferior colliculus of the cat. I. Tonotopic organization, relation of spike counts to tone intensity and firing patterns of single elements. *J. Neurophysiol.* **29**, 288.

Rosen, G. (1958) Dynamic analog speech synthesizer. *J. Acoust. Soc. Am.* **30**, 201.

Rovner, P., Nash-Webber, B. and Woods, W. A. (1974) Control concepts in a speech understanding system. *IEEE Symp. on Speech Recognition*, p. 267.

Sachs, M. B. and Kiang, N. Y.-S. (1968) Two-tone inhibition in auditory nerve fibres. *J. Acoust. Soc. Am.* **43**, 1120.

Sakai, T. and Doshita, S. (1962) The phonetic typewriter. *Proc. IFIP Congress*, Munich.

Samur, M. R. and Rabiner, L. R. (1975) A speaker-independent digit-recognition system. *Bell Syst. Tech. J.* **54**, 81.

Schouten, J. F. (1938) The perception of subjective tones. *Proc. Kon. Nederl. Akad. Wetensch.* **41**, 1086.

Schouten, J. F. (1940) The residue, a new component in subjective sound analysis. *Proc. Kon. Nederl. Akad. Wetensch.* **43**, 356.

Schroeder, M. R. and David, E. E. (1960) A vocoder for transmitting 10 kc/s speech over a 3.5 kc/s channel. *Acustica* **10**, 35.

Shankweiler, D. and Studdert-Kennedy, M. (1967) Identification of consonants and vowels presented to left and right ears. *Q.J. Exptl Psychol.* **19**, 59.

Shankweiler, D. and Studdert-Kennedy, M. (1970) Hemispheric specialization for speech perception. *J. Acoust. Soc. Am.* **48**, 579.

Shannon, C. E. and Weaver, W. (1963) *The Mathematical Theory of Communication*, University of Illinois, Urbana.

Shower, E. G. and Biddulph, R. (1931) Differential pitch sensitivity of the ear. *J. Acoust. Soc. Am.* **3**, 275.

Siegenthaler, B. M. (1950) A study of the intelligibility of sustained vowels. *Quart. J. Speech* **36**, 202.

Singh, S. (1974) A step towards a theory of speech perception. *Speech Communication Seminar* 3, 55. Almqvist & Wiksell, Stockholm.

Slawson, A. W. (1968) Vowel quality and musical timbre as functions of spectrum envelope and fundamental frequency. *J. Acoust. Soc. Am.* **43**, 87.

Stevens, K. N. (1959) Effect of duration on identification. *J. Acoust. Soc. Am.* **31**, 109.

Stevens, K. N. (1960) Toward a model for speech recognition. *J. Acoust Soc. Am.* **32**, 47.

Stevens, K. N. (1968) On the relation between speech movements and speech perception. *Zeitschr. f. Phon.* **21**, 102.

Stevens, K. N. and House, A. S. (1961) An acoustical theory of vowel production and some of its implications. *J. Speech Hear. Res.* **4**, 303.

Stevens, K. N. and Klatt, D. H. (1971) The role of formant transitions in the voice–voiceless distinction for stops. *MIT Quarterly Progress Report* **No. 101**, 188.

Stevens, S. G. D. (1973) Some experiments in the detection of short duration stimuli. *Brit. J. Audiol.* **7**, 81.

Stevens, S. S. (1935) The relation of pitch to intensity. *J. Acoust. Soc. Am.* **6**, 150.

Stevens, S. S. and Davis, H. (1938) *Hearing*, Wiley, New York.

Stevens, S. S., Miller, J. and Truscott, I. (1946) The masking of speech by sine waves, square waves, and regular and modulated pulses. *J. Acoust. Soc. Am.* **18**, 418.

Stevens, S. S. and Volkmann, J. (1940) The relation of pitch to frequency. *Am. J. Psychol.* **53**, 329.

Strevens, P. (1960) Spectra of fricative noise in human speech. *Language and Speech* **3**, 32.

Studdert-Kennedy, M., Shankweiler, D. P., and Schulman, S. (1970) Opposed effects of a delayed channel on perception of dichotically and monotically presented CV syllables. *J. Acoust. Soc. Am.* **48**, 599.

Summerfield, A. Q. and Haggard, M. P. (1972) Speech rate effects in the perception of voicing. *Speech Synthesis and Perception* **6**, 1.

Tamiya, J. and Hiramatu, K. (1958) *J. Acoust. Soc. Japan* **14**, 143.

Tanaka, Y. and Okamoto, J. (1964) Syllable articulation at the time when the trailing edges of zero-crossing waves make random fluctuations. *Memoirs of the Faculty of Engineering*, p. 75. Osaka City University.

Tappert, C. C. (1974) Experiments with a tree search method for converting noisy phonetic representation into standard orthography. *IEEE Symp. on Speech Recognition*, p. 261.

Tappert, C. C., Dixon, N. R. and Rabinowitz, A. S. (1973) Application of sequential decoding for converting phonetic to graphemic representation in automatic recognition of continuous speech (ARCS). *IEEE Trans. Audio Electroacoust.* **AU-21**, 255.

Tasaki, I. (1954) Nerve impulses in individual auditory nerve fibres of guinea pig. *J. Neurophysiol.* **17**, 97.

Teacher, C. F., Kellett, H. and Focht, L. (1967) Experimental, limited vocabulary, speech recognizer. *IEEE Int. Conv. Record.*

Thwing, E. J. (1955) Spread of perstimulatory fatigue of a pure tone to neighbouring frequencies. *J. Acoust. Soc. Am.* **47**, 741.

Tomlinson, R. S. (1966) SPASS—an improved terminal analog speech synthesizer. *M.I.T. QPR 80.*

Tsuchitani, C. and Boudreau, J. C. (1966) Single unit analysis of cat superior olive S-segment with tonal stimuli. *J. Neurophysiol.* **29**, 684.

Turnbull, W. W. (1944) Pitch discrimination as a function of tonal duration. *J. Exptl Psychol.* **34**, 302.

Uldall, E. T. (1971) Isochronous stresses in R.P. *Form and Substance*, p. 205. Academisk Forlag, Copenhagen.

Vartanyan, I. A. (1969) Unit activity in inferior colliculus to amplitude modulated stimuli. *Neurosci. Trans.* **10**, 17.

Walker, D. E. (1974) The SRI speech understanding system. *IEEE Symp. on Speech Recognition*, p. 32.

Wang, W. S.-Y. (1959) Transition and release as perceptual cues for final plosives. *J. Speech Hear. Res.* **2**, 66.

Warren, R. M. (1961) Illusory changes of distinct speech upon repetition—the verbal transformation effect. *Brit. J. Psychol.* **52**, 249.

Warren, R. M. and Obusek, C. J. (1972) Identification of temporal order within auditory sequences. *Perception and Psychophysics* **12**, 86.

Watenabe, T. and Ohgushi, K. (1968) FM sensitive auditory neuron. *Proc. Jap. Acad.* **44**, 968.

Wengel, R. L. and Lane, C. E. (1924) The auditory masking of one pure tone by another and its probable relation to the dynamics of the other ear. *Phys. Rev.* **23**, 226.

Wever, E. G. (1949) *Theory of Hearing*, Wiley, New York.

Whitfield, I. C. (1967) *The Auditory Pathway*, Arnold, London.

Willems, L. F. (1974) Segment oriented speech synthesis by rule. *Eighth Int. Cong. Acoust.* **1**, 294. London.

Wilson, J. P. (1967) Psychoacoustics of obstacle detection using ambient or self-generated noise. *Animal Sonar Systems*, p. 89. Louis-Jean, Gap, Hautes-Alpes, France.

Wilson, J. P. (1973) Psychoacoustical and neurophysiological aspects of auditory pattern recognition. *The Neurosciences: Third Study Program*, p. 147. M.I.T. Press, Cambridge, Mass.

Wilson, J. P. and Evans, E. F. (1971) Grating acuity of the ear: psychophysical and neurophysiological measures of frequency resolving power. *Seventh Int. Congr. Acoustics*, p. 397. Akademiai Kiado, Budapest.

Wilson, J. P. and Johnstone, J. R. (1972) Capacitive probe measure of basilar membrane vibration. *Symposium on Hearing Theory 1972*, p. 172. IPO Eindhoven, Holland.

Winter, P. and Funkenstein, H. H. (1973) The effect of species-specific vocalization on the discharge of auditory cortical cells in the awake squirrel monkey (*Saimiri Sciureus*). *Exptl Brain Res.* **18**, 489.

Wiren, J. and Stubbs, H. L. (1956) Electronic binary selection system for phoneme classification. *J. Acoust Soc. Am.* **28**, 1082.

Woods, W. A. (1974) Motivation and overview of BBN SPEECHLIS, an experimental prototype for speech understanding research. *IEEE Symp. on Speech Recognition*, p. 1.

Author Index

Subject Index

adaptation 78, 84, 85, 87, 88, 124
affricate 3, 4, 11, 45, 54, 55
allophone 51, 55
alveolar 11, 51
analogue threshold logic 109
analysis-by-synthesis 113, 123, 124
anvil 12, 13
auditory theory 122
axon 16

back 3, 6, 40, 44, 68, 69, 77, 83, 105, 109
bandwidth compression 59, 61, 64, 67
basilar membrane 13, 14, 15, 28, 31
Bernoulli 3
bilabial 11
bottom driver 115
bottom-up 116

capacitive probe 18
cardinal 6, 40
categorical perception 80, 82, 121, 123
chain model 91, 92
characteristic frequency 19, 20
close 6, 40, 45, 71
co-articulation 51, 108, 110
cochlea 12, 13, 14, 15, 18, 34, 120
cochlear nucleus 17, 19
cocktail-party effect 102, 104, 124
comb-filtered noise 32
comb model 91, 92, 93
context 44, 51, 86, 101, 111, 121, 122
cortex 17, 19, 21, 22, 84, 85, 120
Corti 14, 15, 16
critical band 27, 28, 30, 68
cross-correlation 105, 109

dendrites 16
diaphragm 3, 5
dichotic 85, 86, 87, 121
difference dimens 24, 25, 26, 73, 74, 82, 89, 108, 120
digital synthesis 63
dimensional analysis 68, 83
diphthong 3, 8, 9, 42, 43, 46, 56, 107
distinctive features 51, 55, 101, 105
distortion 96

duration 28, 29, 40, 42, 43, 66, 71, 72, 75, 76, 78, 81, 83, 89, 90, 91, 92, 103, 111

eardrum 12, 13, 14, 120
electromyographic 122
encodedness 86, 121
endolymph 14
epiglottis 3, 5
error set 111, 112, 116
esophagus 3, 5

fatigue 29, 84, 103, 120, 121
feature detectors 84
foot 91, 93
formant 36, 38, 40, 42, 44, 45, 61, 62, 63, 64, 68, 69, 71, 72, 74, 75, 76, 78, 79, 82, 84, 85, 87, 98, 106, 108, 123
formant synthesizer 61, 62
Fourier analysis 31, 107
Fourier transform 36
frequency discrimination 25
frequency selectivity 18
fricative 3, 4, 10, 11, 38, 42, 43, 49, 50, 64, 79, 83, 90, 98, 105, 106, 114
front 3, 6, 40, 44, 77, 83, 105, 109
function word 116
fundamental 36, 60, 61, 64, 70, 72, 73, 74, 76, 77, 84, 89, 91, 93, 98, 108, 110

glide 3, 4, 9, 47, 75, 106
glottal period 34
glottis 3, 5, 9, 10, 11, 35

hair cells 13, 15, 28, 120
hammer 12
helicotrema 14
hemisphere 17, 85, 88, 121
heterarchical 117, 124
hierarchical 112, 113, 123

incremental simulation 116
incus 13
inferior colliculus 17

137

OTHER TITLES IN THE SERIES IN NATURAL PHILOSOPHY

Other Titles of interest:

MOORE, J. R.: Principles of Oral Surgery
TYLDESLEY, W.R.: Oral Diagnosis
HARMS, E.: Addiction in Youth
RENFREW, C. E.: Speech Disorders in Children
BABINGTON SMITH, B.: Laboratory Experience in Psychology
RODEN, M. S.: Introduction to Communication Theory
SIEGMAN, A. and POPE, B.: Studies in Dyadic Communication